Ghosts of Maryland

Mike Ricksecker

Schiffer Publishing Ltd®

4880 Lower Valley Road, Atglen, Pennsylvania 19310

Cover art: Antietam Battlefield View © Kurt Holter. *Courtesy of www.bigstockphoto.com.*

Other Schiffer Books on Related Subjects
Spooky Creepy Baltimore County, 978-0-7643-3254-8, $14.99
Baltimore Harbor Haunts, 0-7643-2304-0, $14.95

Schiffer Books are available at special discounts for bulk purchases for sales promotions or premiums. Special editions, including personalized covers, corporate imprints, and excerpts can be created in large quantities for special needs. For more information contact the publisher:

Published by Schiffer Publishing Ltd.
4880 Lower Valley Road
Atglen, PA 19310
Phone: (610) 593-1777; Fax: (610) 593-2002
E-mail: Info@schifferbooks.com

For the largest selection of fine reference books on this and related subjects, please visit our web site at:
www.schifferbooks.com
We are always looking for people to write books on new and related subjects. If you have an idea for a book please contact us at the above address.

This book may be purchased from the publisher. Include $5.00 for shipping. Please try your bookstore first. You may write for a free catalog.

In Europe, Schiffer books are distributed by
Bushwood Books
6 Marksbury Ave.
Kew Gardens
Surrey TW9 4JF England
Phone: 44 (0) 20 8392 8585; Fax: 44 (0) 20 8392 9876
E-mail: info@bushwoodbooks.co.uk
Website: www.bushwoodbooks.co.uk

Designed by Stephanie Daugherty
Type set in A Charming Font Superexpanded/NewBskvll BT/Gil Sans

ISBN: 978-0-7643-3423-8
Printed in the United States of America

Dedication

To Toni, Mindy, and Matt...for the "ghost" we created at Grandma and Grandpa's house when we were kids, and to Robin Genelle...you continue to inspire me each and every day of our lives together.

Acknowledgments

The author appreciates the invaluable help and/or inspiration of the following people and organizations:

The Historical Society of Frederick County, the Historical Society of Carroll County, Lorrie Jones, Beverly Litsinger, Don Lady, Beth Cooper of Kansas Ghost Tours, Amy Begg De Groff, Luis Salazar, Chuck Wilson, Donna Metcalf, Beth Tribe, Ruth Vargas, Danny Bouman, Leona McNair, Howard County Library, Enoch Pratt Free Library, the Dr. Samuel A. Mudd Society, Maryland-National Capital Park and Planning Commission, Maryland State Geographic Information Committee, Collin Ricksecker, Arielle Ricksecker, Chase Ricksecker, Cameron Ricksecker, Ren Schuffman, Dinah Roseberry, Ron Angleberger, Lois Szymanski, Gail Ricksecker (for my first ghost book, *Yankee Ghosts*, by Hans Holzer), and my wife, Robin Genelle, without whose continued love and support none of this would be possible.

Contents

Introduction

W hen I first agreed to write this book, I had a dream that I was investigating a haunted house and felt a strange presence near me when I sat down in a chair in a large front hall. I tried to stand up, but the presence kept pushing me back down onto the seat. Finally, whatever the force was gave way and I was able to rise, but it then shoved me toward the front door. My dream self got out of there as quickly as I could.

I believe in ghosts and the supernatural, even inventing ghost stories when I was a kid to explain the creepiness of my grandparents' basement, so with that type of dream kicking off my project I was unsure what to expect as I set forth. My first real experience I can recall was when I was in high school. A friend and I were at a girl's house and she told us a story about how she thought her room was haunted because there was a graveyard out back and no matter what she put on one wall of her bedroom the object would eventually fal! down. We took a look at it and, while we didn't have any problems with things falling off the wall, any time my friend touched the surface he started burning up hot and he'd sweat.

During a business trip in 2006, my supervisor's boss and I had an eerily similar experience on the same night although we were in different rooms at the Peery Hotel in Salt Lake City. We'd both taken off rings before going to bed: he his wedding band and I a nice piece with Australian black opals embedded in the side that I'd picked up when my wife and I had been in St. Thomas. In the morning he discovered his wedding ring unnaturally bent and I discovered one of the opals in my ring broken with a chip missing. My room was right above his and, after consulting with the front desk, we learned that our wing of the hotel was haunted... although this had been the first report of the ghost damaging jewelry.

With these couple of incidents behind me, a desire to know more, and a security in my faith, I was quite eager to explore Maryland's supernatural activity. The result is what you now hold in your hand.

I wanted to make this book a little different than the other ghost books I've read. The first chapter is a brief history of Maryland and why it seems to have been destined to be one of the most haunted states in America. I hold a personal interest in Maryland's history since I have ancestors that were some of the first Germanic settlers in Frederick County in the 1740s (Peter Ricksecker married Elizabeth Krieger whose father was Lorenz Krieger, owner of the farm that is now the town of Thurmont).

I follow that chapter with ten chapters of full-length ghost stories, which take paths both chronologically as well as geographically. I then thought it would be helpful to make *Chapter Twelve* a short text on ghost hunting, a rising practice in today's society with scores of new "hunters" trying to figure out how to start. Finally, instead of just recounting the state's ghost stories, which are many, varied, and more numerous than what anyone could include in a single volume, I wrote *Chapter Thirteen* as an atlas of Maryland ghosts. Broken down by county with appropriate maps and descriptions, I think you'll find it very useful in tracking down Maryland's most famous spirits. There are over one hundred included in this book!

I also hope you enjoy some of the historical aspects I've incorporated throughout the text. Maryland is rich in it, but some of these spirits had been reduced to a single line of recognition in modern stories and ghostly website blurbs. For example, Ariana Calvert's tale in *Chapter Two* had been shortened to the spirit of a young girl who was forbidden the one she loved. Sources nearly one hundred years old described a much deeper story.

By the way, during my travels, I discovered the grand front hall from my dream greatly resembled the central passageway in Montpelier Mansion in Laurel, although I did not attempt to sit on any of the furniture while there.

1

Maryland...
A Haunted State

Maryland is rife with supernatural activity and is considered one of the most haunted states in the country. Nearly every town across every county in the Old Line State has an eerie tale to tell. From the Eastern Shore to Garrett County, Marylanders have been reporting ghosts and spiritual activity for centuries. Perhaps this is because Maryland's origins are shrouded in death.

George Calvert, generally considered the "father" of Maryland, once served as England's principal secretary of state in the early seventeenth century, but he had his heart set on colonizing the New World and a land where Catholics and Protestants could thrive together. Calvert was a favorite of King James I, but he'd converted to Catholicism in 1624 and Catholics were forbidden from serving in high political positions in England at that time. The following year, after Calvert revealed his faith, the king granted him his wish, bestowing upon him the title of Lord Baltimore and giving Calvert land in Newfoundland. After the death of King James that year, his successor, Charles I, offered to retract Parliament's oath of religious supremacy if George would retain his position. Calvert declined and left for his new land.

He called this home the rather charming name of Avalon, but after experiencing a harsh northern climate and hostile French attacks, he abandoned it and traveled to Virginia. There he met hostility of a religious nature, so, leaving his wife and servants behind, he returned to England seeking a new land grant just north of the Potomac River near the Chesapeake Bay. Tragedy struck in 1630, as a ship sent to retrieve his wife sank in the chilly waters off the coast of Ireland and she drowned. Later that year, Calvert's household contracted the plague, although he survived the notoriously fatal disease. Finally, in 1632, King Charles granted Calvert the land he sought and named it Maryland in honor of his queen Henrietta Maria. However, five weeks before the charter was sealed George Calvert suddenly died.

It was under that ominous mark that Cecilius Calvert, George's son and the second Lord Baltimore, accepted the charter in his father's stead. Cecilius tasked his brother Leonard with organizing an expedition and settling the land put in the charge of his family. Cecilius remained in England and never actually stepped foot in the New World, although he didn't pass away until 1675.

While Maryland may have had an inauspicious founding that possibly contributed to the state's mysterious nature, its Civil War history certainly cemented its place in notoriety. Numerous battles and skirmishes erupted within a state that was considered part of the Union, but had many more Southern sympathizers than Northern. Maryland was forcibly held in Union control because it, in conjunction with Virginia, surrounds Washington D.C., to the point that the guns of Fort McHenry were actually pointed at the city of Baltimore to keep Southern sympathizers at bay. The bloodiest one-day battle in American history was fought in Maryland at Antietam, and thousands of wounded soldiers from Gettysburg were carried over the border to be treated in Maryland where they later died. It is also through Maryland that John Wilkes Booth and his accomplice fled after assassinating President Abraham Lincoln, leaving a number of puzzling and still highly debated tales along the way.

The Maryland Monument at Antietam National Battlefield.

Throughout the state, many local legends and ghost stories contain the sighting of a Civil War soldier or something akin to the sounds of heavy boots up a back stairwell being attributed to a soldier who died in the vicinity. Some reenactments at old battlegrounds are actually performed by the spectral combatants themselves. Even treasure hunters roam old trails seeking out treasures that were hurriedly buried while troops were under attack.

With Maryland's checkered past and its historical foundation, it's not surprising many of the lost souls of her past continue to try to tell their part of the tale.

2

Mount Airy Mansion and Plantation

Mount Airy Mansion, located in Rosaryville Park near Upper Marlboro, Maryland, is one of the oldest haunted estates in Maryland. The most archaic part of the structure was originally a hunting lodge built around 1660 by Charles Calvert, the third Lord Baltimore, when he arrived from England. At that time the lodge consisted of one large room some fifty feet in length, with a fireplace pitted at each end, and was used by the Lords Baltimore in this fashion for some time until the grounds evolved into a plantation.

In 1751, Charles, the fifth Lord Baltimore, gave the plantation and 9,200 acres of land to his son Benedict. Unfortunately, a year later the estate suffered the first of two major fires and the cause was believed to have been arson.

Repaired, the storied plantation hosted the wedding of George Washington's stepson John Parke Custis on February 4, 1774 to Eleanor "Nellie" Calvert. At the outset, our first president was opposed to the marriage because he believed the bride and groom to be too young. He eventually relinquished his stance and was on hand for the wedding in what is now the Calvert Room and the proceeding two-week long wedding

Mount Airy Mansion in Rosaryville Park. The brick structure on the right is the old hunting lodge.

celebration. Afterward, Washington was a regular visitor to Mount Airy Mansion, and it is believed he gave the Calverts the boxwood at the front of the house.

The residence remained in the hands of the Calvert family until 1903, when Eleanor Calvert died and the house and the furnishings were all auctioned. The new tenant, Matilda "Tillie" Duvall, turned the estate into an upscale restaurant known as Dower House, and it was known to have entertained Presidents Taft, Wilson, Coolidge, and Hoover. Dower House continued in operation until a 1931 blaze sunk the business.

Following the fire, editor-publisher Eleanor "Cissy" Patterson of the *Washington Times-Herald* bought Mount Airy, restored it, and proceeded to add a swimming pool, tennis court, guest cottages, and a large greenhouse for her favorite collection of orchids. She loved to entertain, inviting over guests that included Franklin and Eleanor Roosevelt, Robert Considine, and Adela St. John. Although she had many other homes, Mrs.

Patterson often visited Mount Airy Mansion and died in her bedroom there in 1948.

She left the estate to Ann Bowie Smith and, in 1973, the State of Maryland purchased the mansion and grounds from the Smith family to make it a part of Rosaryville State Park. Due to inadequate funding, the house was left to disintegrate for ten years, but in the 1980s the house went through four years of restoration work. Mount Airy Mansion and Plantation now serves as an event center for weddings, music, and the arts, but it is not only earthly guests to which the estate plays host.

Calvert Family Ghosts...

Tales of hauntings at the Mount Airy Mansion have been floating around for so long that London's Society for Psychical Research sent investigators to the estate back in the 1930s.

Once used by the Lords Baltimore, the hunting lodge is connected to the rest of the house.

Their research unearthed the spirit of Elizabeth Biscoe Calvert, which wanders the unlit halls at night searching for a cache of hidden jewels lost long ago. However, the tale of why she may have hidden these jewels has been lost to time. Fortunately for us, Mount Airy has a plethora of ghosts haunting the premises from which to study.

There's the ghost of Ariana Calvert, a distraught young woman, heartbroken and mourning, about the house, still desiring a forbidden love she was disallowed to have in life. Her father did not like her suitor and banned her from seeing him, but Ariana patiently waited for her father's heart to soften. When it became clear that his daughter could not stop thinking of the young man, Benedict Calvert sent her to Annapolis to live with her sisters and find a suitor there. She politely refused every single one. Ariana's health began to fade from depression, and when her father died, her mother took pity and finally gave consent for the girl to marry her love. However, it was too late and the girl passed away from her condition. Ariana's morbid soul still carries on at Mount Airy, longing for the man of which she'd been deprived.

The last Calvert to live in the mansion, Miss Eleanor Calvert, brutally died in 1902 at the age of 81. She was in the habit of carrying an old oil lamp with her at night, which a number of family members had warned was not a safe practice. One dark night it tipped in her hand as she was walking down the stairs. Her clothes lit up in flames and she fell to her death as she frantically tried to snuff out the fire. Eleanor had been a rather eccentric old woman who insisted on keeping the parlor doors locked. Her body was laid out the night before her funeral in that very same parlor, but the next morning the doors to the room were found closed and locked. After much searching and the key nowhere to be found, a decision was made by the family to break into the parlor. Those there were astonished when the key was found inside the parlor resting on a table next to Eleanor's coffin.

Tillie Duvall had a number of creepy experiences with the ghosts of the mansion when she ran Dower House. According to an account in John Martin Hammon's 1914 tome *Colonial Mansions of Maryland and Delaware*, "There is the time when with her husband Mrs. Duvall drove back from Washington, one dark night, and found a solitary horseman in the garb of a hundred years ago calmly sitting his horse in front of the door, at the end of the long aisle of trees. By the dim light of the stars they saw him inspecting them with a gaze, as if to say, 'What do you want here?' and then he vanished." Mrs. Duvall also witnessed doors opening and closing on their own, beds sagging and creaking with no living person in them, and a dining room in which no light would burn and a fresh candle brought into the room would be extinguished. Her most frightening experience came one night when she awoke to the apparition of a pale woman hovering above her and sliding her cold hands around Mrs. Duvall's throat. This may be the same spectral woman that has reportedly floated to each room at night and awoken whomever may be sleeping there. Or it could be another ghost entirely.

Renovation of the old estate in the 1980s seemed to stir up a few curious spirits as well. Arriving early one day at about 7 a.m., one worker saw a man in a red shirt standing in a second story window. He was amazed at the sight because not only should no one have been in the house at the time, but there also was no floor on the second level yet on which the person could stand. Two other men working after hours witnessed a door opening by itself. They checked the hinges and re-closed it, but it then eerily opened itself a second time. They fled from the site and vowed never to work at Mount Airy after dusk again.

Mount Airy Mansion and Plantation is a beautiful example of colonial architecture and life...*as well as the afterlife*. As one of the most haunted houses in all of Maryland, it's a window into another world that time won't soon let us forget.

3

The Snowden Homes

One of the wealthier families in Maryland during the eighteenth and nineteenth centuries was the Snowden family of Welsh decent. Richard Snowden, who arrived in 1669, not only made a profit in agriculture, but was also part owner of a successful ironworks that lasted numbers of generations. There are at least two noted occasions in which George Washington ordered iron implements from Snowden's Ironworks for his estate at Mount Vernon.

As the Snowden family's wealth grew, so did their land holdings. At one point, Major Thomas Snowden, Richard's grandson, owned over 9,000 acres in Prince George's County, much of which is now the towns of Laurel and Beltsville, as well as the surrounding area. Throughout the county there are a number of former Snowden estates and homes that were built on this land and are now either being restored by private owners or are being run by the Prince George's County Department of Parks and Recreation.

Montpelier

One of these estates is Montpelier Mansion, a Georgian-style mansion built between 1781 and 1785 by Thomas. Two fireboxes in the house are inscribed "TSA 1783," indicating ownership by Thomas and his wife Ann Ridgely Snowden. The mansion originally overlooked the Patuxent River, but the creation of the Rocky Gorge Dam to feed the local reservoir now blocks the river from continuing to flow past.

Chronicler Lawrence Buckler Thomas once wrote of Thomas Snowden, "He lived at Montpelier which was on the great Northern and Southern Post-road, and entertained great numbers of people who were then continually passing upon it, and in accordance with the hospitable customs of the day, would not hesitate to stop at his residence for the night. Washington, himself, once spent the night there, and the bed in which he slept is still preserved."

Approaching Montpelier Mansion from the garden terrace.

Unfortunately, our first president's inaugural stay at Montpelier wasn't a pleasant one. He spent the night there in May 1787 en route to Philadelphia as a member of the Continental Congress. He was suffering from a severe headache as well as a stomachache, and reportedly went to bed early. He returned a second time on his way back from Philadelphia without incident.

Martha Washington also spent the night at Montpelier in 1789 on her way to attend the inauguration of her husband as president in New York. Another president's wife, Abigail Adams, also spent the night at the mansion while traveling south to join her husband in Washington in 1800.

Apparently, the hospitality of the Snowdens' has continued on in the afterlife. It has been said that the ghosts of George and Martha Washington have roamed the grounds at Montpelier, and there have even been sightings of Thomas Jefferson.

From the central passageway below, a ghostly woman wrapped in a quilt has been known to walk up the stairs.

Aside from our forefathers, in 1968, a caretaker spotted the apparition of Anne Ridgley in the house, recognizing her from the Snowden artwork. Another caretaker at the mansion, while he couldn't name anyone specific, stated that he has seen figures moving about in the east wing.

A former tour guide at Montpelier Mansion had a number of ghostly stories to share. At nights during the autumn, Thomas Snowden's son has been known to ride up to the house on horseback. An unidentified woman wrapped in a colorful quilt has walked up the main stairwell from time to time and has disappeared into the wall. On occasion, she may walk through a person or even look directly at him or her. An apparition of a young girl has sometimes been spotted in an upstairs window outside the master bedroom. There is also a ghost of a prankster, one who likes to lock doors and cabinets. Sometimes a faint smell of roses can waft through the air of rooms that contain no flowers.

Oaklands

Oaklands, an older home in the Snowden lineage, has an even larger collection of strange tales surrounding it. The majority of the brick home was built in the 1780s, but its foundation dates to an older structure (built in the 1730s) upon which the current house was constructed. Tradition holds that Richard Snowden built the 1730s house as a wedding present for his daughter. A recent examination of the plaster in an upstairs bedroom has revealed a layer also dating to the 1730s, so the origins of the building remains shrouded in mystery.

What is known for sure is that Oaklands was passed down by Major Thomas Snowden of Montpelier to his son, Richard, when Richard married Eliza Warfield in February 1798. After the death of Eliza, Richard married her sister Louisa. Ann Snowden, the eldest child of Richard and Eliza, inherited the property and married Captain John Contee, a Marine Commandant who served on the *USS Constitution* during the War of 1812. Her younger brother, Richard Nicholls Snowden, was a participant in one of the most infamous card games in Maryland folklore.

One dark night a heated card game was being battled in the sitting room between Richard and three others. The stakes were high and the players were rife with red wine when one of them was suddenly called away from the game by an urgent message. His departure would spell the end of the game.

Richard and the two other guests declared, "We would play with the Devil if he took your place."

A few moments after the player left, a knock resounded from the door and a tall, slim man whom no one recognized entered.

"May I take the vacant place?" he offered.

The host was anxious to continue the game, so he let the stranger sit with them at the table. Heated play resumed and the newcomer was fixed in an incredible streak of luck. They played on through the morning, into the following afternoon, and were still going strong into the evening...the four of them unwilling to end their boisterous game. Finally, the stranger had won every last dollar of the other three men sitting at the table, and he rose to bid them farewell. At the door he bowed, and the weary eyes of the three men sharpened when they noticed the outline of a forked tail beneath the back of his coat and the scent of brimstone that wafted in the air when he swept out of the house.

Ann and Richard's father was buried with his two wives, Eliza and Louisa, somewhere on the premises of Oaklands. Their brother Thomas was buried there as well, but over time the site of these graves has been lost. When the land around the house was recently sold to a housing developer, archaeologists were brought out by the county to try to locate the graves and make sure they weren't disturbed during development. All the archaeologists were able to find were the charred remnants of an old barn. Preservationists have suggested that since many of the Snowdens were Quakers there may not be grave markers since Quakers often didn't make marking graves a practice. It's also possible that the grave markers simply crumbled away

Loaded with ghost stories, Oaklands is currently under renovation.

over time. While Oaklands is officially designated as a historic Prince George's County site with a cemetery, the location of the Snowden graves is still a mystery.

In 1911, the property came into control of Charles R. Hooff, whose wife was a descendent of the Snowdens, although no longer of the direct line. Prior to his acquisition, Oaklands had fallen into a state of disrepair and Hooff's goal was to renovate the house as close to the original specifications as he could. In the 1920s, John W. Staggers bought the rejuvenated estate and his descendents continue to own it to this day. Their account of events at Oaklands has ranged from what some might call a "typical" haunting to rather extraordinary.

It's been commonly reported that between 9 and 10 p.m. the sound of horse hooves gallop up the driveway. The gallop will stop at the front door and will be followed by the sound of footsteps entering the house. Not long after, the sound of the horse hooves will resume, galloping off into the night.

Could this mysterious rider be the ghost of the "Devil" that came to play cards? Or could it be the messenger that called away one of the players from the game? It could be the ghost of Richard Contee whom, according to the wife of John Staggers, many family members claimed to have seen walking the grounds on numerous occasions. Richard Contee was a Major in Robert E. Lee's Army of Northern Virginia during the Civil War. There's a strong rumor that Major Contee had gone insane and, during one of his "episodes," had carved his name into the wall of one of the third-floor bedrooms. To this day, the etching of his name can still be seen when the sun shines on it just right.

Another common occurrence at Oaklands is the sudden strong scent of apple blossoms wafting through the air. The current owner in the Staggers lineage, Donald Lady, is a skeptic concerning ghosts, but he did confirm that the apple blossom smell is a popular story and he once experienced something similar — a strong scent and the feeling that he wasn't alone. When asked what type of scent he smelled, he responded, "Let's put it this way... what a non-smoker may call apple blossoms, a smoker would call a strong scent. But it was definitely out of place."

A variety of apparitions has been seen in and around the house. A small boy in a brown suit with an old rounded collar has been spotted a few times in an upstairs bedroom. No one is certain who he may be, although there has been speculation that he is the son of Major Contee. There have also been sightings of a large, black woman and a black man wearing vintage work clothes. It's unknown who they may specifically be, but at one point there had been nearly two hundred slaves working at Oaklands. A woman in a hoop dress has reportedly been seen in the middle of the night, and an old woman peering out of a third floor bedroom window has been seen at various times of day.

One such incident with the old woman in the window also involved Mr. Lady. He was driving up to the house when his passenger remarked that there was someone in the left most third-floor window. The house was closed at the time for renovation and no one should have been in the house. Fearing trespassers, they ran inside, but no one was to be found and no entry point into the house was discovered. When Mr. Lady later asked his friend whom he saw, he answered that it was an old woman who was at the window for just a moment.

John Pecor and Pam Pecor Unger are grandchildren of John Staggers and have both lived in the house for significant periods of time. Pam had heard the invisible horse hooves approaching the house several times and seen the ghosts of the slaves. She often encountered the apple blossom scent and would occasionally hear the sound of a rocking chair creaking back and forth in the bedroom above hers. When she encountered the ghost of the small boy, he simply stared at her and refused to go away until she turned off the bedroom light. Pam also had a unique haunting of her own. Whenever she would begin to take a bath or shower, an unseen entity would begin ringing an old farm bell just outside the house. To eliminate the annoying disturbance, Pam removed the bell.

Pam's husband, Bill, was once awakened in the middle of the night by the sound of heavy footsteps dragging across the floor. He couldn't see anything in the darkness, but the sound of breathing kept drawing ever closer to him. Finally, he could feel someone bending over him, but still there was nothing to be seen. Bill felt paralyzed and wanted to shout but couldn't. After what seemed like an eternity, the presence still pressing down on him, Bill was able to gather enough of himself together to poke Pam who was fast asleep next to him. When she sprang awake, the terrifying entity instantly dissipated.

While the incident with Bill may have been one of Oaklands' more terrifying incidents, John Pecor has probably experienced one of the more unusual. He was outside on the house grounds when a lovely young woman in a long dress motioned to him from across the lawn. He was interested to find out what she wanted though she said nothing to him and just began walking. She led John to one of the terraces and pointed down toward the ground. When she did so, she disappeared. John was shocked, but when he peered down to where she had pointed, he discovered a gold chain, most likely a necklace, but of unknown provenance. He took it to a local Laurel jeweler who dated the piece to craftsmanship of the 1700s. John saw the woman again at a later date, but it's unclear as to who she is and what her connection to the chain may be. Was this a ghost seeking a missing heirloom? Or was the chain some sort of connection to a transgression committed against the woman, as John and Pam believe?

The brother and sister have both on a number of occasions heard a woman crying within the house, although an exact location could never be pinpointed. They, as well as others, have also heard screams emanating from the nearby woods — the site of an unsolved murder that took place over seventy years ago. Those who have heard the screams believe they are from the woman who was killed there.

While the majority of the strange events at Oaklands have been eerie and sometimes terrifying, there have been signs of another light recently. Don Lady has been renovating the old house and spent some time praying as to whether or not it was the right thing to do. A few nights later he had a roaring fire going in the fireplace. It had become so hot that the protective grating he had placed in front of it had started warping and melting. He pulled the searing metal away and put out the fire. The following day he was on the phone with a friend and was excitedly telling her about a 1950s vintage chandelier that he found in the house when his excitement grew even more. Resting upon what had been a melting grate was a small white plastic cross...something he knows couldn't have been there the night before because it would have easily melted. Was it a sign from God? Why not... after all the Devil had already been at Oaklands playing cards?

Ghosts of Westminster

Historic Westminster in Carroll County is bustling with spectral activity. Originally founded in 1764 as Winchester for William Winchester, it was renamed Westminster to alleviate its popular confusion with Winchester, Virginia. During the Battle of Gettysburg, the town was a vital supply depot for the Union Army, but it is now a college town where students come to attend McDaniel College. The guided ghost tours through downtown have become so popular that there is now a self-guided version available via a brochure.

Cockey's Tavern

Although it's unclear precisely when the building was constructed in the early 1800s, the first reference to the two-story house being used as a hotel and tavern came in 1832 under the operation of Joshua Cockey. Within a few years, Cockey tried his hand with an inn in Baltimore and his interest in the Westminster property was sold off by 1841.

Cockey's Tavern reopened under the care of the Historical Society of Carroll County in 2009.

The building changed hands over the years, serving many times as a residence. It underwent a temporary name change to Hoffman's Inn after Frank and Mary Hoffman purchased it some time after 1922. Together, they ran the old tavern as a boarding house and eatery until 1969. The proprietors that followed the Hoffmans returned the title to Cockey's Tavern until they folded after an arson fire ruined a substantial portion of the back of the building in 2000. It was then purchased by the Historical Society of Carroll County and restored, finally reopening in 2009.

During its thirty-year jaunt as the modern and upscale Cockey's Tavern, patrons and staff have witnessed a variety of hauntings. Heavy boots were often heard tramping up and down the stairs, and many suspected this was the ghost of an old Civil War solider since Confederate troops had once made Westminster's Main Street a temporary headquarters. If one shouted up the stairs for the stomping to stop, the noise would cease. This same ghost is also credited with rattling the glasses and bottles around the bar. One time when waitresses were closing up, they had gone through each room snuffing out the candles. When they were about to leave, they looked back and all the candles on the mantle had been re-lit.

Pictures appeared to be the ghost's forte. Once, when a woman from Baltimore was meeting with a friend in the tavern, she remarked that she didn't believe in ghosts. A picture on the wall behind her promptly fell and hit her in the head. The wire on the back of the picture was not broken and the woman responded with, "I believe!"

Mr. Walsh, a local lawyer, used to eat at Cockey's Tavern nearly every day and he always sat at the same table. Staff opening the restaurant one morning found the painting of General Grant that hung over the fireplace resting face down at the spot in which Walsh normally sat. Again, the wire was not broken and the place setting at the table was not damaged. It was later learned that Mr. Walsh had passed away that previous night.

This same picture of Grant may have recently resurfaced. After the 2000 fire, the contents of Cockey's Tavern were auctioned off. The grandson of the man who bought a painting of a bearded man at the auction recently gave the painting to the Historical Society to hang at Cockey's Tavern once again. Former employees remarked that they used to believe the painting was of Ulysses S. Grant, but now many have their doubts. However, the painting still has remnants of the dark marks that resembled blood pouring out from the man's sleeve and thumb. These marks originally appeared on the painting one day in the old tavern seemingly out of nowhere and have now spread to the figure's head.

Since the renovation, the ghostly activity seems to have quieted down, but it is still present. A recent paranormal investigation in 2009 detected the spirit of "Albert" on the third floor, a teacher who is likely to have lived there while Cockey's Tavern was Hoffman's Inn boarding house during the early twentieth century.

The Fiery Furnace

Legh Master was a cruel, rich widower who moved to Carroll County after losing his wife in England. Through the blood of hard-worked slaves, he established a very productive iron furnace and increased his fortune. With business thriving, the area popularly became known as Furnace Hills.

Still longing for his deceased wife, he dressed up properly and attended many church functions in Westminster, but no woman would give him a second look. Frustrated, he pushed himself on a slave girl who had her heart set on another slave named Sam, but when she didn't comply Master had the girl beaten. When Sam found out, he tried to kill Legh Master with a shovel. At that treachery, the angered owner bound up Sam, fired up the furnace, and had the slave thrown in by his fellow workers. Some say that there are nights in which Sam's spirit returns to Legh Master's house at Avondale to haunt the old home.

The slave girl mysteriously disappeared and rumors spread that Master had bricked her up alive in the kitchen oven. During the 1930s, a fire decimated parts of Avondale's kitchen and when it was put out, the firefighters tore out a few bricks from the chimney to check for possible causes. They were intrigued when they discovered an iron gate behind the brick. More of the brick was torn out to uncover the gate, and when it was

The cracked grave of Legh Master.

opened they found an old hidden oven. Within that oven were human remains.

Dying at the age of eighty, Legh Master's funeral was unattended, but that didn't stop his legend from growing. Although he was buried the customary six feet underground, his bones kept rising out of the earth. After this happened a third time, his remains were moved to Ascension Church to be secured by a large slab of stone. However, even the large stone has suffered and is scarred with a large split as if the bones beneath have tried to break out.

Locals say that on dark and windy nights, one can spot the ghost of Legh Master riding between New Windsor and Westminster on a dark gray horse, breathing fire. The procession is said to be led by a madly dancing imp clutching a lantern, with Legh Master on his steed crying out for his lost soul.

Headless Tom

On the bitter cold night of Christmas Eve 1844, Big Tom Parkes sat alone in his cell without a single visitor to wish him well. Arrested for the fourth time in four months for disturbing the peace, visitors of other prisoners shied away from Tom's cell, afraid he may try to provoke something while they visited with loved ones. With nothing to do, Tom sat quietly in his corner cell and listened.

The sheriff was at a loss as to what to do with Big Tom. Tom Parkes was a large, strong man and it had been a struggle to haul him into the jail, taking three men to drag Tom to the cell. The sheriff worried that the jail wouldn't be able to contain Parkes and wondered out loud whether he should send the prisoner to the Baltimore Penitentiary. Unhinged at the idea of spending time in a high-security prison, Big Tom killed himself on Christmas Day, getting a hold of something sharp enough to slice his own throat.

In an odd twist, a phrenologist (one who studies the bone structure of the head in relation to psychological and intellectual traits) by the name of Dr. Zollickhoffer was called to the jail to take a look at Tom. He was enamored with the specimen provided by Big Tom's cranium and removed the head to perform research. The rest of Tom's body was buried in a local cemetery.

To this day, it is said that Big Tom Parkes still roams the old jail, headless and hands outstretched, in search of his missing body part.

Opera House Ghost

Marshall Buell, a comedian from Alabama, exhibited a poor choice in topic during his performance at Westminster's Odd Fellows Hall in the late 1860s when he began cracking anti-Union jokes and poked fun at President Ulysses S. Grant. A number of audience members who sided with the North were so offended that they began throwing rocks at the comedian. One actually hit Buell in the chest, but he kept performing. The sheriff was called upon to handle the situation, and three spectators shouting insults at the comedian were hauled out of the building.

After the performance, a shaken Buell hurriedly packed all of his belongings into a heavy trunk so he could set out toward his next performance in Hagerstown. The sheriff sought him out to make sure he was alright, and Buell told him how these men had been following him since Alabama, likely paid to terrorize him because of the message he was delivering through his comedy. The sheriff offered to protect the comedian in the jail overnight and then would see him off the next day, but Buell refused. Alone at the back of the Odd Fellows Hall as he prepared his horse, Marshall Buell was attacked from behind and his throat was slit from ear to ear.

After the Southerner's demise, townsfolk began whispering about the odd sight sometimes seen in the back lot of the hall. The apparition of a headless body would appear out of thin air and begin what seemed like a mouthless monologue, gesturing with its hands as if it was telling jokes. Some reported seeing the full figure of Marshall Buell mouthing silent performances from the stairs. Today as the restored Opera House Printing Company, employees tell of strange happenings from within the historic building, odd

Odd Fellows Hall is now the Opera House Printing Company in downtown Westminster.

footsteps, and the opening and closing of doors; however, the comedian hasn't given a performance from the back lot in some time.

5

Downtown Frederick

Historic downtown Frederick is teeming with ghosts and the supernatural. Surveyed and laid out by Daniel Dulany in 1745 and settled by German immigrant Johann "John" Thomas Schley the following year, Frederick was a strategic crossroad connecting the northeast to settlements in Virginia and other southern colonies, as well as the western frontier. Numerous dignitaries have been through this city including George Washington, Abraham Lincoln, Robert E. Lee, Benjamin Harrison, Harry Truman, and Winston Churchill. This type of cross-traffic still holds true to this day as a number of highways and state routes cross paths here in varying directions; however, Frederick is also a spiritual crossroad.

One of Dulany's first priorities for the town was to establish churches, and he accomplished this by donating a lot between Patrick and Church Streets to the Evangelical Reformed Church. German Lutherans who had been living in the Frederick area since the 1730s also built a church on East Church Street. Likewise, in 1747, the Maryland Assembly authorized a tax on all parishioners of All Saints Parish to raise three hundred pounds in order to buy three acres in Frederick for the construction of a church building. Churches would later play a role in a number of Frederick's paranormal tales.

Orphan Tales

The Historical Society of Frederick County located in downtown Frederick contains a bevy of information about the city's formative years and its role in the Civil War, but it was also once the site of the Loats Female Orphan Asylum. Originally built in 1820 by Dr. William Baltzell, the house has only had three private owners, including Colonel Alexander Baird Hanson and John Loats; upon Loats' death, it was willed it to the Evangelical Lutheran Church. It was the church that turned the house into an orphanage in 1879, and it served in this capacity until 1958. The expanding Historical Society of Frederick County bought the building in 1959.

The interior of the old home is constructed in a rather majestic Federal tradition, including King of Prussia mantels in a double parlor, top hat dormers, a balcony overlooking the rear garden, and a grand central hall with matching entrances on either end. It's in this stylish fashion that the orphaned girls lived and, according

The Loats Female Orphan Asylum is now the Historical Society of Frederick County.

to many diaries, actually lived a rather spirited existence until the age of eighteen, quite unlike many other orphanages of the period that were run poorly. Perhaps it's those fond memories that have enticed the ghosts to return and relive their lives.

One of the Historical Society's most famous ghosts is that of a woman in a white dress that has been encountered on many occasions. She's said to have her hair tied up in a bun and the dated style of clothing is out of the late 1800s with a high collar and long sleeves. Who she may be, no one knows for sure; some suspect it may be Lizzie Kreh, a former singing instructor, seamstress, cook, and even headmistress. She has been seen on a number of occasions wandering the corridors and sitting in an antique rocking chair.

Other hauntings of the old orphanage include trunks moving around on their own and the sound of "Avalon" being played from an old phonograph. The phonograph, it is said, is a quite challenge to get working by hand and no one is in the room when it starts to play.

Civil War Ghosts

Also prominent in Frederick's paranormal tales is its role as a crossroad during the Civil War. Troops from each side marched through several times, a Union military hospital was constructed here in 1861, there was a heavily used rail depot in Frederick, and just south of town was the site of a battle.

In July 1864, Confederate troops, led by General Jubal A. Early, poured into Frederick as part of a planned invasion of Maryland by General Robert E. Lee. This was to be a precursor to an invasion of Washington D.C. and a lure to draw Union General Ulysses S. Grant from his pressing advance on Richmond, Virginia. Although residents of Frederick fled, businesses closed, and banks withdrew their money, a letter from General Early was delivered to the Mayor of Frederick demanding flour, sugar, coffee, salt, bacon, and $200,000 in cash. In fear of their lives, city officials responded quickly and were able to get the banks to disburse the needed funds. Stacks of bills were delivered in baskets by wagon to the Confederate army. What happened to the money after that is a mystery, as there is no record of the Confederates spending it. Some believe General Early may have pocketed it for himself. Frederick and Maryland's congressional delegation have formally sought repayment from the U.S. treasury ever since.

The request and obtainment of the money became a curse for the Confederate army. The time it took the city to round up the funds was enough for Union troops to organize a line of defense and further delay Confederate troops from marching south to Washington. Although the Union lost the ensuing Battle of Monocacy, General Grant was able to fortify Washington and General Early diverted to Poolesville, Virginia, a key tactic that worked in the North's favor during the war, although many souls were lost.

The Legend of Barbara Fritchie

Another Frederick Civil War legend — that of Barbara Fritchie — has held fast throughout the years, with her former home becoming a popular tourist attraction in downtown Frederick. She gained notoriety as an American patriot during the Civil War when southern troops led by General Stonewall Jackson marched through Frederick. In defiance of their occupation, Barbara is said to have hung her head out of a window and waved the Union stars and stripes at the troops. John Greenleaf Whittier memorialized this event in 1864 with a poem that bears Barbara's name. An excerpt follows:

"Shoot, if you must, this old gray head,
But spare your country's flag," she said.
A shade of sadness, a blush of shame,
Over the face of the leader came;
The nobler nature within him stirred
To life at that woman's deed and word;
"Who touches a hair of yon gray head
Dies like a dog! March on!" he said.

— *Yale Book of American Verse*, 1912

The curtains are drawn back upstairs in the Barbara Fritchie house, awaiting the Frederick icon to peer out the window yet again.

Unfortunately, the event didn't happen as described. History tells us that Jackson's troops marched south down Bentz Street (known as Mill Alley at the time) and turned west onto Patrick Street. To march in front of Fritchie's house along Patrick Street, Jackson's troops would had to have turned east from Bentz and crossed Carroll Creek. A letter from former Frederick mayor John Engelbrecht, a man who lived across the street from Mrs. Fritchie for thirty-six years, tells us that General Robert E. Lee's troops stopped in front of their houses while Jackson's troops marched through. Mr. Engelbrecht saw no flag waving during the time that Lee was stopped outside, and he confirmed that Jackson's troops marched west. Another Patrick Street resident, Samuel Tyler, agreed with Engelbrect's account, but also suggested that the halting of Lee's troops may have been meshed with another incident involving flag waving. When General Jesse Reno, the Union general killed at the Battle of South Mountain, once passed by with his troops, a little girl with Barbara Fritchie held a flag out the window. *The Baltimore Sun* and *New York Times* published both of these accounts in 1875. However, the truth of the matter shouldn't taint the significance of Barbara's folklore. The poem by Whittier inspired the Union troops to victory during a time of national upheaval.

While mysteries abound about Barbara Fritchie's legend in life, mysteries also abound about her legend in death. On numerous occasions Barbara's personal effects, which are displayed at the Barbara Fritchie House and Museum, have gone missing only to be found again in odd places elsewhere around the house, most notably under the bed. A slide projector that tells the story of Barbara Fritchie's life will start up and always stop at Barbara's picture...no matter where in the presentation the slide had been placed. A number of workers have reported a mysterious indentation of a person of Barbara's stature left in her bed. They will straighten it out only to find the indentation back hours later. One worker has even seen an apparition of Barbara, a quilt from the bed draped over ghostly white legs as she rocked in an antique rocker.

National Civil War Medicine Museum

Some claim that downtown Frederick's most haunted site is the National Civil War Medicine Museum on East Patrick Street. The building was used as a funeral home and undertaker's establishment for nearly a century, but during the Civil War it became something more. Frederick already housed General Hospital #1 for the Union army, and at one point some 9,000 injured swarmed the town. However, since this undertaker was located right near a local train depot, dead bodies from the war would be dropped off to be embalmed after the battles of South Mountain and Antietam, and then they would be shipped right back out later on the train, creating a gruesome procession in and out of the building.

Thousands of visitors—*both living and dead*—have entered the doors of the National Civil War Medicine Museum.

Since the museum has moved into the building, the ghosts of the War Between the States have seemed to fit right in with the relics on display. The stomping of heavy boots on hardwood floors that no longer exist have been heard throughout the building and sometimes screams emanate from the camp scene. A volunteer once spotted a young teenager in dated clothes on the second floor looking at one of the displays. The air chilled to the point that one's breath would crystallize and the volunteer suddenly realized the boy was talking, but nothing he was saying could be heard. Other shadowy figures have been detected over the years, but another apparition was seen during one of the local ghost tours. A trembling woman insisted she had seen a pale bearded face staring at her from one of the building's top floor windows—*after hours*—when no one was in the museum.

Other Downtown Haunts

Gaslight Antiques

Located at 118 East Church Street, across from St. John's, Gaslight Antiques was once a boarding house, but it is now a private residence. It is also suspected that the location may have once been used for the Underground Railroad during the early nineteenth century since there is a tunnel that leads from the basement of this home under the street to the church. It is now bricked over, but the ghostly sound of Latin chanting sometimes emanates from the area.

During the height of its business days, an unwed woman in her 40s gave birth to a child while staying at the boarding house, but, unfortunately, the baby soon died. The woman was so distraught that she hung herself from the balcony. Since then the woman's spirit has haunted the house by repeatedly trashing the kitchen, throwing pots, pans, and dishes about the place.

Other unexplained hauntings of the house include the heavy footsteps of a man and the disembodied laughing of two women.

Weinberg Center for the Performing Arts

The Weinberg Center for the Performing Arts in downtown Frederick was originally the Tivoli Theater, Frederick's high-class theater built during the Roaring Twenties. Amenities included crystal chandeliers, plush velvet rocking chairs, mosaic tile floors, and marble columns. Even the staff was impeccable with managers dressed in tuxedos and ushers wearing uniforms faceted with gold-buttons. A Wurlitzer pipe organ that is still there to this day was prominently featured and the Tivoli had the distinction of becoming Frederick's first air-conditioned public facility. The $100,000 compressors were sort of a gift from Jack Warner of Warner Brothers, which owned the Tivoli. In a chance meeting

The Weinberg Center for the Performing Arts is home to a ghost named Jimmy who worked there when the building was the Tivoli Theater.

with the studio executive, Dr. Eddie Thomas, a friend of Walkersville horseman W. L. Brann, advised Warner to bet on Brann's horse, Challedon. Warner won big on the bet and, discovering Dr. Thomas was a regular at the Tivoli, installed the air-conditioning as repayment.

On October 9, 1976, after nearly a week of rain, the banks of Carroll Creek were breached and downtown Frederick was flooded. Fortunately, there were no reported deaths, but there were some injuries, cars were washed down streets, and the Wurlitzer organ floated up to the stage from where it rested below. President Gerald Ford declared the city a disaster area and the city was granted $5 million in disaster relief, but the total to repair the damage exceeded $25 million. The flood nearly spelled the end of the Tivoli.

Interest in the theater had already been on the decline as popularity in television increased and multiplex theaters began springing up. Demolition of the building was considered after the 1976 flood, but the community came together and raised $175,000 to restore the Tivoli. The Weinberg family, which had owned it since 1959, decided to donate the theater to the City of Frederick, and it re-opened on February 9, 1978, under the name the Weinberg Center for the Performing Arts. Today the Weinberg Center showcases a wide range of dramatic, musical, artistic, and educational programs.

The resident ghost of the Weinberg Center is said to be Jimmy, a former projection operator who died of a heart attack. Jimmy doesn't like new employees working at the old theater and will often make a mess of the bathrooms when one is hired. He's been known to vandalize vending machines after hours as well, and strange power outages have even been attributed to the spirit. Many have felt Jimmy's presence from behind when walking within the Weinberg, but one person realized he was never bothered again after a time in which he was walking out of the theater and he simply stated, "Good night, Jimmy."

The Patapsco Female Institute and Mount Ida

The Patapsco Female Institute

Looming atop Ellicott City's highest elevation are the remnants of what was once the Patapsco Female Institute (PFI), one of the best known schools for young American women during the nineteenth century. Led by Almira Hart Lincoln Phelps, students studied natural sciences, history, languages, music, and art. Mrs. Phelps believed that young women should learn how to earn a living rather than attend a typical finishing school of the day. Many graduates became teachers and a number of the women took on the management responsibilities of plantations when their husband went off to fight in the Civil War. Mrs. Phelps retired to Baltimore in 1856 after the violent death of her daughter in a train accident, but would return often to visit and offer advice.

When public schools first came into existence, many private schools experienced heavy losses in students, but PFI held its own for a long time, especially under the

The stoic columns of the Patapsco Female Institute.

leadership of Sarah Randolph, granddaughter of Thomas Jefferson, during the 1878–1881 period. However, when the competition with public schools finally took its toll and the building started falling into disrepair, the Board of Trustees voted to extinguish the existence of the Patapsco Female Institute.

After the school closed in 1891, this granite Greek Revival structure featuring four Doric columns was used as the Berg Alnwyck Hotel, a residence, a World War I convalescent hospital, a nursing home for the poor, and a summer outdoor theater. During the 1950s, the site fell into ruins after years of neglect. In 1967, the Howard County government purchased PFI and restoration of the site began in the 1980s. Today it is open for tours, Victorian teas, summer theaters, and day camps.

For two weekends at the end of the season in October, the park opens for a special Halloween scare event. This is quite fitting given the eeriness of the architecture in the dim light, but it's also possible that a real specter from the past may scare patrons of the Halloween event.

Annie Van Delot was the daughter of a rich Southern plantation owner and she was quite open with her displeasure with the school. She was far from home in an isolated area and was displeased, as were most of the girls, with the way sanitary conditions had degraded. Heating was poor, and a number of the young women developed influenza and croup. Annie, however, developed pneumonia during her first winter at the school in 1879 and died.

The spirit of Annie lives on at Patapsco Female Institute and has been seen many times, usually in a white dress. Before the site was restored, children sledding in the winter on the steep slopes would sometimes spot Annie leaning against a nearby tree, forlorn and watching them. Today, a number of visitors have reported spotting her sullen image about the grounds, and more sensitive individuals have been known to speak with her. Poor Annie is still awaiting the arrival of her parents to take her away from the confines of PFI.

Mount Ida

From Private Residence to Visitor Center

The Mount Ida Visitor Center, just down the hill from the Patapsco Female Institute, serves as the office for the historic park. Designed by famed architect N. G. Starkweather, it was constructed by PFI builder Charles Timanus for William Ellicott, grandson of one of the founders of Ellicott's Mills. It was the final home built by an Ellicott within the town's limits and it only ever served as a residence until it was transformed into a historic visitor's center.

Miss Ida Tyson lived at the home well into her nineties until she passed away, and many believe it is her spirit that haunts the house. In life, although she required a cane to

Ida Tyson's old home is now a visitor's center.

move about and used an ear horn to aid her hearing, she was a lively person with a great interest in children. In death, some have come to call her "The Cleaning Ghost" since she still works to maintain the upkeep of the house she loved to keep pristine. It's rumored that the custodial staff doesn't even venture upstairs to clean because they know that Ida's ghost has already cleaned there. The keys that she was fond of carrying can be heard at times jingling throughout the house and sometimes a rocking chair will begin rocking on its own. It seems Miss Ida is just as lively as she ever had been.

7

The Hayden House

Some ghosts, apparently, still have an appetite for food although they no longer have a body with which to consume it. How does a ghost grabbing a midnight snack digest its food? At this point, we don't know, but we do know that the ghost at the Hayden House in Ellicott City is quite a chef.

Edwin Parsons Hayden was best known as the first Clerk of Howard County Court; he served from 1847 until his untimely death at the age of 39 in 1850. He studied law at Yale and began his practice at what was then known as Ellicott's Mills in 1836. Four years later he built a granite home at Oak Lawn near the Court House. In 1847, he won a seat in the Maryland Legislature after running on the Whig party ticket, but only served a few months prior to his appointment by the Governor as Clerk.

Hayden took ill in May of 1850 and lost a battle with congestion of the lungs on the tenth of that month. He left his wife, Elizabeth, and six children alone at Oak Lawn.

In the 1870s, the family sold the house to Henry A. Wooten, Esq., after which the house passed in and out of the hands of a number of private owners. The building has been home to both the Howard County Board of Education and the District Court, and is now occupied by the Howard County Circuit Court Law Library. A difficult house to find—almost a ghost of its own

The term "last meal" isn't in the vocabulary of the ghosts at the Hayden House.

of sort—the structure has become almost entirely engulfed by the Circuit Court with only the front façade still visible from the outside. It's very easy for one to walk past it and not even realize the old Hayden House at Oak Lawn is right there.

Reports of ghostly activity at the old home were at their highest in the 1970s, when the house served as the District Court and the regional Division of Parole and Probation office. Clerks would be deep into their work when the lights would suddenly flick on and off, startling them. At times the sound of footsteps would creep by them with no visible owner to the treading. In what may actually be considered a helpful gesture, the office coffeepot would begin heating for no apparent reason...even if it was actually unplugged. The mysterious haunting of the coffeepot, however, was only a precursor to other strange activities.

The unusual aroma wafted down the hallways of the offices, out of place and out of time. It didn't matter the time of day that the scent would begin its trek throughout the building. An administrative assistant in the morning or a clerk working overtime at night would begin smelling bacon and eggs, arousing their stomachs. Sometimes soup was the special of the day and their stomachs would rumble for lunch. The only problem with all of this was that the old home was bereft of kitchen appliances. There was absolutely no way anybody could be cooking at any time of the day! After a while, those working within the old Hayden House began referring to the unusual smells of food as "the cooking ghost."

A judge's administrative assistant explained one incident, "Over in the Willow Grove Jail, just a stone's throw from the circuit court building, the aroma of salty, smoked bacon being fried to a crisp floats into the second floor offices of the old, gray, granite structure. I envision a bacon, lettuce, and tomato sandwich this time of day, but the jailhouse cook says that she isn't cooking bacon or anything else, just cleaning up the kitchen. But the smell of mouth-watering bacon is still coming into the office, and the ghost continues to cook!"

The cooking ghost at Oak Lawn apparently also likes to arrange table settings for the food it prepares. One sultry night, a staff member had turned on an air-conditioning unit that blew across a table that had been brought in for an office party the following day. As the air blew he witnessed a number of napkins unfolding and refolding themselves against the current.

The culinary arts may not be this ghost's only hobby or... there may even be *other* ghosts within the home. People opening the building in the morning have reported seeing a figure through one of the panes of glass in the front door. A search of the house after opening always revealed nothing. Those working at night would become nervous in anticipation of what the darkness would bring. All too often they spotted a chair rocking by itself in someone's office. One district court commissioner often worked alone late and usually felt the presence of someone else around.

The old Oaklawn home has been consumed by the court house.

One night around 4 a.m., he was in the process of transferring money from the house to one of the other buildings and was at the safe when he heard an odd noise resonate from behind him. Fearing an intruder, he stepped out into the hall and looked about. All was still for a moment...and then suddenly...the storage room door slowly opened. He crept up to the door, discovered no one was there, and bolted from the building.

During another late night, this same court commissioner was traversing the stairs up to the second floor when he paused on the landing. Out of the corner of his eye he saw a white cloud of smoke billowing over the staircase. It was like a dense ball of mist yet opaque as he could still see some of the wall behind the apparition. When he turned to confront it, the white essence quickly disappeared.

A more recent account from 1997 tells us there may be more to the manifestation than a mystical white mist. A former security guard related that he spotted the ghostly form of a woman near one of the upper floor front windows. In his account, he stated that the woman appeared to be busy cooking. It is still unknown who this woman may be.

8

Lilburn Castle

Up the narrow, winding College Avenue in Ellicott City looms the stoic Lilburn, built in 1857 by Henry Richard Hazlehurst and most recognized by its parapet-adorned tower. It's an ideal location for a house of its nature, overlooking the Ellicott City historic district like a hilltop castle guarding the countryside, battlements at the ready. Given the political climate at the time, that may not be far from the truth. This restored twenty-room granite mansion, complete with a bell tower, carriage house, cottage, and one of Howard County's only three-story smoke houses, has become known to many as the most haunted house in Maryland.

Henry Richard Hazlehurst was a mechanical engineer who partnered with B & O Railroad Master of Machinery James Murray to build steam fire engines for Baltimore and marine engines for the United States Navy, when he built Lilburn. He would later make his fortune in the iron industry during the Civil War, after which he settled into farming on his seven acres of land. His wife Elizabeth, known to friends and family as "Lizzie," was a devoted lover of flowers and spent much of her time designing arrangements in the gardens lining the estate.

Unfortunately, the Hazlehurst family spent a significant amount of time grieving the loss of loved ones at Lilburn.

Some say Lilburn Castle is the most haunted house in Maryland.

Lizzie, as well as several of their children, died rather prematurely in life, and it has long been believed that one of their daughters died in childbirth at Lilburn. Henry outlived the majority of his family and passed away in 1900 at the age of eighty-five.

The first signs of paranormal activity at Lilburn Castle were reported after the John Maginnis family moved into the Gothic mansion in 1923. The most common occurrence they encountered was the sound of footsteps heard within the ominous tower that once stood at the back of the house where the battlements now rise. When noises began emanating from other locations around the mansion, the residents began believing that the ghost of the Hazlehurst daughter who had died in childbirth had returned to haunt her childhood home, tormented that she lost her life before experiencing raising her baby. These rumors began circulating around town and the legend of Lilburn spread.

There was much more to talk about around Ellicott City when Lilburn nearly burned to the ground one holiday season from a Christmas tree fire. Most of the original structure was destroyed although, fortunately, nobody perished in the blaze to add more souls to future hauntings. However, the hauntings escalated after Maginnis rebuilt the mansion and decided to replace the old tower's steeped roof with the current parapets. Reports of strange sounds and occurrences from this area of the house increased and caused people to speculate that Henry Richard Hazlehurst had returned from the dead in defiance of the architectural change.

More of the same was reported about Lilburn for years until Sherwood Baldersons purchased the mansion in the 1960s. It was under Baldersons' watch that reports of supernatural activity began to transcend that of previous generations. The family dog was particularly tuned in to the forces at Lilburn, visibly afraid in the mansion and refusing to go near a small room along the second floor hallway. While unusual sounds that had always been reported, such as footsteps, continued to be commonplace, new brands of eeriness began to take place.

Lilburn Castle's parapet-adorned tower has large casement-style windows, which had problems staying shut. Tired of repeatedly closing the tower windows, Mr. Baldersons, in an act of desperation, tied down the windows from the inside with rope. When he traversed outside to examine his work from the mansion grounds, he was aghast to discover that the ropes had been loosened and the windows opened. The tower windows would remain a perpetual problem for years, something unseen insisting they remain open.

Another notorious incident occurred during a dinner party hosted by the Baldersons'. They had organized a social event for a number of friends and, as the evening waned, many of them began remarking about the crystal chandelier swinging about in the dining room. They were distressed at the action of the chandelier since there was no breeze of any sort to propel it, but the Baldsersons' chalked it up to another haunting by one of their resident spirits.

It seems the ghosts of Lilburn also had a particular affinity for the Baldersons' housekeeper. On a number of occasions she told stories of hearing a child crying and of smells emanating from the library that resembled cigar smoke although no one in the mansion smoked cigars. She's also the only person to have reported seeing apparitions at Lilburn. The housekeeper described how she had once seen the ghostly image of a small girl in a chiffon dress roaming one of the mansion hallways. During another incident, the spectral form of a man actually tried to prevent her from entering a room and she had to force herself past it in order to get by.

The parapets of Lilburn loom behind the old home.

The Baldersons' eventually sold the mansion to Dr. Eugenia King, who lived there for a number of years with her son Jeff. During their stay, they reported a number of the same strange occurrences as the Baldersons'. Dr. King had identical problems with the tower windows as Mr. Baldersons...closing them only to have them opened by unseen hands. The dining room chandelier also swung about on its own from time to time as it had during the dinner party. The ghosts of Lilburn did pull out a new trick one time when a vase of flowers started pouring itself out without warning right in front of Dr. King. Perhaps gardening enthusiast Lizzie Hazlehurst didn't approve of the doctor's floral décor. Eugenia sold the mansion in 1983.

Since the time Dr. King sold Lilburn, the mansion has been in and out of a number of hands. The Whitney family purchased the house in 1983, investing considerable time and money restoring the castle. Julie Whitney claimed that their family never experienced any supernatural occurrences and that her initial fear of living there was simply due to the morbid state of disrepair of the structure. However, the Whitneys only stayed in the mansion until 1988. In 2005, Thomas and Debra McGinty, who had just bought the property the year prior, revealed plans to turn Lilburn into a four-bedroom bed and breakfast, utilizing two rooms in the main house and two rooms in the external cottage. Conditional use was approved by Howard County in February 2006, but, in a strange turn, the mansion was put up for sale again that October. By summer 2007, new owners had moved in, and the mysteries of Lilburn Castle were ready to be passed on yet again.

The Surratt House and Tavern

On the night of April 14, 1865, in part of a conspiracy, renowned actor John Wilkes Booth shot and killed President Abraham Lincoln at Ford's Theater in Washington, D.C. He leaped from the balcony, caught his foot in the bunting, and broke his leg as he crashed to the stage floor. During his flight from the scene of the crime, he and David Herold made a stop at Surratt Tavern, a known safehouse for the Confederacy during the Civil War.

A tavern, an inn, a post office, a polling place, and a home, the structure now known as the Surratt House was built in 1852 when John H. Surratt bought 287 acres of the surrounding land from Charles B. Calvert in Prince George's County at the intersection of Marlboro-Piscataway and New Cut roads. This crossroad, which included a livery stable across the street, was an ideal location for John to set up his business. The small pub, which was a part of the main household, was a rather energetic meeting place where the local farmers and small businessmen could get a drink, have a smoke, or even take in a meal while conversing with friends and travelers. A room on the second floor served as an inn for those passing through at night.

Although he waited outside one fateful night in 1865, John Wilkes Booth is *not* one of the ghosts at Mary Surratt's house.

Unfortunately, John H. Surratt died a young death during the early morning hours of August 26, 1862, mostly likely suffering a heart attack. His wife, Mary, was left in quite a predicament. John had amassed a degree of debt with a number of uncollected tavern bills. Slaves began to run away from the farm and life for Mary Surratt became a mess. In October 1964, she rented the house to John Lloyd and she began running a boarding house at 541 H Street in Washington, D.C. This is where her family met John Wilkes Booth and where much of the Lincoln assassination was conspired between Mary's son and Confederate secret agent John Surratt and George Atzerodt, David Herold, Lewis Powell, and Wilkes Booth.

Close to midnight on the night of April 14, 1865, John Wilkes Booth and his accomplice, David Herold, stopped off at the Surratt Tavern on their flight out of Washington to grab supplies. John had arranged hidden weapons in the tavern's attic, carbines hanging by ropes between the studs in the walls.

Upon retrieval, one fell down to the first floor and proved to be damning evidence when it was later found. Field glasses were also made ready for Booth when he and Herold arrived. Mary's tenant at the Surratt Tavern, John Lloyd, testified against Mary that she had requested him to make these things available. After their brief stop, Booth and Herold continued forth to Dr. Samuel Mudd's house to deal with Booth's broken leg.

The fallout for the Surratt family was heartbreaking. Mary was convicted in the Lincoln Conspiracy trial and hanged July 7, 1865. In an unfortunate twist, there had been a pending case in the Supreme Court regarding the jurisdiction of the military court in civilian cases, a case that was resolved less than a year after Mary's death. Due to her trial under military jurisdiction, Mary Surratt will always be the only woman in American history ever executed at the gallows.

John Surratt, Jr. was allegedly spying for General Edwin Lee in Elmira, New York, at the time of the Lincoln assassination. He fled to Canada and remained there until after his mother's death more

Mary Surratt at the gallows July 7, 1865. *Courtesy of Library of Congress.*

than a year later. He was finally arrested in Alexandria, Egypt, in 1866, and was brought back to the United States for trial. He was released in 1868 after his case resulted in a hung jury in a civil trial. Of those involved in the Lincoln assassination, John Jr. was the last to pass away, succumbing to pneumonia in 1916.

Four years after Mary's execution, her daughter, Anna, pleaded with the federal government that Mary's remains be returned to the family. She was successful, but the grave marker at Mt. Olivet Cemetery in Washington, D.C., still rings ominously with the simple inscription, "Mrs. Surratt."

The Surratts' house was sold and the contents liquidated, so the original furnishings are long since gone. Now operated by the Maryland-National Capital Parks and Planning Commission (MNCPPC), the old house presently maintains a painting of Mary hanging in the hallway, but most of the current furnishings are donations from the time period.

Otherworldly activity at the Surratt house was first reported during the 1940s and 1950s. A widow who owned the home rented half of it out and a number of the tenants claimed to have seen the spectral image of Mary lingering on the staircase landing between the first and second floors. Other tenants often heard disembodied voices emanating from the back of the house when they were alone.

After the MNCPPC acquired the residence in 1965 and began their historical preservation and tours, other strange stories began to surface. Some of the earliest phenomena included more sightings of spirits from the beyond. While once moving a group from one bedroom to another, a tour guide felt as if she had left someone behind. When she went back to check her intuition, she discovered a young girl in Victorian clothing straightening out the bedspread and then peering under the bed as if she were looking for something she'd lost. At first the tour guide didn't understand what she'd seen and started heading back toward the group to find the girl's parents. Once the girl's appearance brought a realization to the guide that her clothing was out of place, the tour guide looked back, but the young girl had disappeared. Could this have been an image of Anna?

The same bedroom has had other visitors as well. Another tour guide's teenage daughter was once startled when she saw a man's reflection in a wall mirror. He was large and bearded, and casually sitting in an old rocking chair. When the girl turned her head to look at the man, he wasn't anywhere to be seen and the image in the mirror disappeared.

The most common experience at the Surratt house are the sounds of footsteps echoing from the past around the house. Tourists have on a number of occasions, from the first floor, heard the sound of footsteps above them when there were no other groups on that level. Guides and workers at the house who have had more time to observe the footsteps describe ones on the first floor as the thud of heavy work boots that move from one end of the house to the other. While downstairs in the tavern area, a lighter set of footsteps has been heard overhead from the bedroom. Similar footsteps have also been heard out in the hallway of the second floor while others still had been heard in one of the rooms on that level.

On rare occasions, the smell of tobacco will waft throughout the house...even though no one is present to smoke or chew it. While there are a few plugs of tobacco kept around for tours, they are generally put away. Also, the spittoons in the tavern area are showpieces and are not used in this present day, so there is no explanation for the smell.

During a recent investigation of the house, a medium was brought in. Without being told the history of the house and the people who had lived there, she didn't pick up much with her senses...until she entered Anna's room. There she stated that she was being overwhelmed with a feeling of great sadness. A number of people were disappointed in the singular result, hoping for confirmation of the previous reports. However, the medium asserted that her experience may not be definitive. It has been widely suspected that some ghosts and spirits do end up moving on and that many hauntings are "seasonal," meaning they may be active for a while and then go through dry spells without any. Perhaps another season of sightings of little girls in Victorian dresses and men in rocking chairs is coming yet again.

Impression at the Mudd House

The chill of the night air flooded the old farmhouse at the ungodly hour of 4 a.m. on April 15, 1865. The strange man at the door claimed he was looking for medical attention for his friend, Mr. Tyler, who had broken his leg. Hesitant at first given the odd hour of the call, Dr. Samuel Mudd ushered the two men inside and, in the process, ushered in a complete change in the course of his life.

"Mr. Tyler" was not the man's name. This was, in fact, John Wilkes Booth, and the United States authorities were hunting him. The man who had knocked at the door of the Mudd house in Charles County was Booth's accomplice, David Herold, and they were both wearing makeshift disguises. They had just ridden south on horseback from the house of Mary Surratt and her son, John, where they had picked up supplies for their flight out of Washington, D.C. Booth couldn't ride much longer with the leg misplaced from his jump out of Ford's Theater's balcony, where he'd shot Abraham Lincoln, and Mudd's house was on their way out of Maryland. Mudd had previously met Booth, but later claimed that he did not recognize the man that morning.

The doctor set Booth's leg in an upstairs bedroom and tended to his basic needs. After a short amount of rest and recovery, Booth and Herold vacated the farmhouse that afternoon with Mudd pointing the way to Parson Wilmer's, their next destination.

Three days later, Lt. Alexander Lovett, an investigator in the Booth escape, called upon the Mudd house to inquire about the man. Mudd insisted that the man whose leg he fixed was a stranger to him, although there were a handful of accounts in which the two had met. Mudd later claimed that on that fateful night Booth was wearing a cloak over his head, a heavy shawl, and bore a mustache.

On April 21, Lovett returned to search the house. There was nothing to be found except for an old boot, which one of the servants had tossed under the upstairs bed. This was the boot Dr. Mudd had cut off Booth's broken leg; it bore the inscription "J. Wilkes ---."

Mudd was taken into custody at Carroll Prison and soldiers surrounded the house while Booth was still at-large. In her own words, Mrs. Sarah Frances "Frankie" Mudd described the scene at the farmhouse when her husband was first taken away:

The Samuel Mudd House is becoming more infamous today for its ghosts than for its legendary past.

"A few days later a company of soldiers were stationed on our farm. They burned the fences, destroyed the wheat and tobacco crops; pulled the boards off the corn-house, so that the corn fell out on the ground, and all the corn that the horses could not eat was trampled under their hoofs in such a way as to render it unfit for use. The meat-house was broken open and the meat taken out. All that they could not eat was left scattered on the hillside where they had pitched their camps. A day or so after their arrival my husband's sister came over to see me. She wanted some garden seeds, and asked me to go down with her to the old gardener, Mr. John Best, to get them for her. When we went out no soldiers were in sight. We carried a basket, and the old man tied up some seeds in packages, put them in the basket, and then asked us to go to see his garden. A few moments after we entered the garden we were surrounded by soldiers. One officer came over and demanded to know what we had in the basket. The little packages of seeds were unwrapped, the contents examined. With a crest-fallen look he remarked, 'I thought you were carrying food to Booth.'"

On April 26, 1865, Booth was caught and killed, and the regiment at the Mudd house vacated the premises. However, Samuel Mudd still remained in custody and was tried in the conspiracy of the Lincoln assassination. His life spared by only a single vote, he was convicted and sentenced to life in prison at Fort Jefferson in the Dry Tortugas, Florida.

In 1867, there was a massive outbreak of yellow fever at the prison, which also claimed the life of the prison doctor. Mudd assumed the role and worked hard to get the situation under control. It almost claimed his life, but he was able to treat the sick and set up an environment that allowed the epidemic to subside. For his heroics, President Andrew Johnson pardoned him in 1869.

Dr. Mudd returned to his home in Maryland and lived out the remainder of his years there until he died of pneumonia in 1883.

Almost a century later, Mrs. Louise Mudd Arehart devoted much of her time and effort to restoring and preserving the old Mudd farmhouse while other family members sought to clear Dr. Mudd's name. At her own house in La Plata, Mrs. Arehart had begun hearing knocking at her front door, but when she answered, no one would be there. The sound of footsteps could be heard going up and down the stairs in her hall, and soon after she began seeing the appearance of a man around the property of her house. This figure was always seen in black trousers and white shirt with a vest, the sleeves of the shirt always rolled up to his elbows. On one particular occasion, Mrs. Arehart nearly ran into the man in her house while she was busy putting away silverware — she passed him through the doorway leading into her dining room. Frightened of the intruder, she fetched her dog and took it throughout the house to try and find the man, but he was nowhere to be found. After pondering for some time, Mrs. Arehart finally realized who the man was...her grandfather, Dr. Samuel Mudd.

At this revelation, Mrs. Arehart became convinced that Dr. Mudd had returned in concern over the state of disrepair his old home had fallen. She persuaded her brother, Joe, who still farmed the land surrounding the home, to let the farmhouse be turned into a museum. With the help of local politicians, she organized the Committee for the Restoration of the Samuel A. Mudd House and it became listed on the National Register of Historic Places in 1974. In 1983, it finally opened to the public...and eerie tales have emanated from the house ever since.

Common disturbances at the home include unanswered knocks at the door, disembodied footsteps around the house, and several sightings of Civil War soldiers. A doll in the upstairs bedroom has reportedly flown out of the chair where it normally sits. The room in which Booth stayed has had reports of coughing emanating from it when no one was there, and periodically an impression can be seen in the bed as if someone was lying there. On one occasion, the door to the attic in the upstairs hallway flew open and a strong gust of wind ripped through the second level. Even Mrs. Mudd has been seen looking out one of the windows of the old home.

In autumn of 2008, a group of Civil War re-enactors were camped around the house when they noticed the artificial candles in the windows of the house were still illuminated. A few of them went inside to put out the candles by loosening the bulbs, but when they returned to their positions, they noticed the lights were still on. They went back and removed the batteries from the candles, but a half-hour later the candles were illuminated once again.

That same season the author's thirteen-year-old daughter had a strange experience at the house. According to her, "The tour guide was showing us some pictures that were hanging up on the living room wall when all of a sudden I felt something pounding under my feet beneath the floor. It was as if someone was knocking at the door, only my feet were standing on the door. Then when we were out back looking at the tombstone, I was just thinking of how nice the breeze was when it felt like the ground lifted from my foot. Someone pushed from underneath the ground and made my foot go up, then they just let go and my foot went flying down."

A return trip was even more revealing... I had lost my original photographs of the house so my wife suggested we make a day trip out there even though she hadn't been feeling well. Much to our dismay, the gates were locked when we pulled up, as we had not realized we'd ventured out on a day the house was closed. However, our timing couldn't have been more perfect. A truck pulled up next to us and one of the staff got out to open the gates. He invited us up since he was already giving a private showing later on.

We explained to him my dilemma with the photographs and he invited us inside while he opened the house. While

The bed impression left by a ghost in the room where John Wilkes Booth slept.

heading upstairs, I asked him what sort of experiences he'd had in the house and he explained that he frequently had to fix impressions of a body on one of the beds, had seen Mrs. Mudd staring out of one of the upstairs windows a few times, and on one occasion he heard the voice of Henry Mudd talking to him.

While he tended to the windows in the room where John Wilkes Booth had slept, I looked down at the bed and was nearly floored. "So this is one of the impressions?"

He spun about and his face flushed when he saw that I was pointing at a human-sized impression sunken into the left side of the bed. "See! That's what I'm talking about!"

I asked to take a few pictures, which he granted, but he remained visibly agitated. "It's not like this when we leave the house at night. Then we have to come up here and fix it to make sure everything looks good for the public."

I was ecstatic with the find. It certainly looked like someone had been lying down on his or her side on the bed, with elbow and feet impressions clearly visible. The whole time, however, my wife had remained downstairs, almost unmovable from the small entrance hall. She later told me that she hadn't wanted to venture any further into the home because of how unnaturally cold she felt just standing there near the base of the stairs.

Outside near the tombstone, the staff member related some of the previously told stories to us and admitted that the attention has been a bit overwhelming. A number of paranormal societies have been out to the farmhouse and *TAPS Magazine* had recently spent three days investigating Dr. Mudd's old home.

Of note, the Dr. Samuel A. Mudd Society, a private institution of his decedents that operate the house, maintains that the phrase, "his name is mud," is not a reference to Dr. Mudd and was in use long before the Lincoln assassination.

11

Ghosts of Charles Street

Not all ghosts pre-date the twentieth century, and two fine Baltimore establishments on Charles Street have more modern tales to tell. Club Charles and the Zodiac Restaurant share the same city block, are owned by the same person, and...both have ghosts. However, the demeanor of their spirits, similar to their histories, are like night and day.

Club Charles was a popular nightspot during the Roaring Twenties, an era of social exhilaration and illegal alcohol, but it was dry and kept its business clean. The Zodiac, on the other hand, housed a speakeasy, serving banned spirits during prohibition. Together, they provided a corner Baltimore with energetic nightlife for a number of years.

Club Charles

The social haunt that stood at the location of Club Charles during the 1920s was re-opened as the Wigwam Restaurant in 1951 under the direction of Esther West. The restaurant was immediately successful, but over the years the neighborhood began to decay. Esther held her own, refurbishing and renaming the establishment Club Charles in 1981. It has since become a popular nightspot once again.

The resident ghost at Club Charles is fondly known as "Frenchie" in death as he had been in life. Born Edouard Neyt near Paris, France, in 1925, Frenchie served as a spy during World War II. When the war ended, he immigrated to Baltimore and began waiting tables at upscale restaurants such was Miller Bros. and the Harvey House. He frequented Club Charles after his shift ended and was the consummate prankster and ladies man. For quite a while he rented out a room above the bar, dying there of acute alcoholism in 1979. He has remained at Club Charles and continues to play his pranks on a nearly daily basis.

As a spirit, he still makes his appearances at Club Charles in his customary waiter's tuxedo and most patrons and staff are quite enamored with his antics. When he's seemingly "thirsty," he will turn on a tap of beer, but he doesn't place a glass underneath, allowing the drink to flow out to the floor. He's also taken a bottle of beer out of an ice chest and set it up on the bar with a glass to be poured. One of his favorite past times is to rearrange the carry-out liquor bottles. Every night they're straightened out and arranged in a specific order, but usually the next day they're found in disarray. Frenchie also likes to play tricks with the glasses, dropping them, but catching them and placing them on the floor gently without breaking. He's also toyed with the phone more often in recent years. There's a phone in the club that does *not* take incoming calls, but he will cause it to ring and to continue ringing even when someone has picked up the receiver.

Not everyone, however, has been pleased with Frenchie's playfulness. Local pub lore tells of a group of policemen and cab drivers who used to hold regular card games for a number of years at Club Charles while Frenchie was still alive. When the waiter would get off his shift, he would have fun with the players by messing with their hair or trying to sit in their laps. The playful harassment didn't stop after Frenchie's death, with many in the group insisting they could feel the ghost disturbing their hair. One of the policemen got so angry one time he pulled out his gun, fired a shot into the ceiling, and shouted, "Damn it, Frenchie! Leave my hair alone!"

While having so much in common, the ghosts of Club Charles and the Zodiac Restaurant are very different.

Zodiac

The ghost next door in the Zodiac, however, is of a different ilk. A local resident who had been around since the Prohibition era stated that a man named McKim had run the old speakeasy. One year, after his wife left him, Mr. McKim hanged himself in the basement of the building. It is this story that makes locals believe the dapper man in the pristine white linen suit frequently seen throughout the restaurant before he suddenly disappears is Mr. McKim. His likeness is so human at times that while sitting at table number 13, waiters will actually place a menu before him. When they return to take his order, they are astonished that he is gone. He has also been known to appear on the third floor and those traversing the stairs to that level have sometimes felt a push, nearly falling down the flight of steps. Many on staff have outright refused to go up there. Doors slam loudly at the Zodiac, and most who have witnessed the ghost and his hauntings truly feel that he is an unhappy spirit.

Unfortunately, the Zodiac recently shut its doors in August 2008 due to a gas line break caused by construction on the street, but its owner would love to reopen the popular restaurant. Whether the troubled ghost would like to welcome guests again is another matter.

12

Ghost Hunting

Ghost hunting has risen in popularity in recent years. Once a practice conducted mostly by mediums, paranormal investigators, and teenagers looking for a good scare in an old house, ghost hunting is now more open to even the simply curious. It has gained traction through television shows and magazines, opening people's minds to the possibility of what may be out there in a world that is generally unseen to the human eye. Organizations and groups like the Maryland Ghost and Spirit Association headed up by Beverly Litsinger have become more commonplace, and there are even Internet radio stations now dedicated to the paranormal and feature such broadcasts as Lorrie Jones' and Tara Deters' "Ghost Chicks."

Training in parapsychology is advisable, but a simple search through Internet message boards reveals small pick-up groups forming across the nation to ghost hunt. Lorrie and Tara didn't start actively ghost hunting until a chilling weekend at the Myrtles Plantation in St. Francisville, Louisiana—a bed and breakfast considered one of the most haunted locations in the United States—propelled them into the field. They have since received paranormal investigative training at the HCH Institute in Lafayette, California, under the tutelage of Professor Lloyd Auerbach and have run dozens of investigations.

There are two fundamental types of defined methodologies in this field. A ghost "hunt" is a basic visit to a site with the intention to witness a ghost and possibly attempt to capture it on film or audio recording. A ghost or paranormal "investigation" is much deeper. Not only will the investigator try to capture the ghost or spirit on film and audio, but he or she will also conduct interviews, take down notes, and make other recordings such as temperature and electromagnetic readings. With either method, it's generally accepted that smaller groups are better than larger ones since the energy of a large group can overwhelm whatever spirit may be present.

The first rule of thumb in ghost hunting is to be skeptical. Just because something odd is going on in a house doesn't necessarily mean a ghost is present. Lorrie Jones tells the story of a girl who thought she had a ghost because a television that worked in one room wouldn't work in another. When Lorrie asked the girl to have her father test other appliances in the outlets, they discovered faulty wiring. "She was actually bummed that she didn't have a 'ghost,' but she could watch MTV again," Lorrie said.

Ghost hunters are not licensed investigators in any sense of the word. They are not above the law and must respect the rights of others just like any other citizen. In other words, if there is a "No Trespassing" sign, then don't trespass. Receive permission from the owner of a property before entering, but if he or she declines, then leave politely. If confidentiality is requested, respect that as well.

If the ghost hunter or group is given permission to enter a potential location, it's advised to do so with some sort of spiritual protection. This may be done in the form of a prayer or chant, whichever the group chooses, and should be done again upon exit. Bev Litsinger, a paranormal investigator and psychic medium, has been interacting with spirits her entire life and will leave a location if she gets a bad feeling about it. "It can follow you home," she says, "and some are mean." Her cat has gotten upset on numerous occasions after Bev has walked in the door...as she'll often arrive home with something that tagged along.

There are various devices on the market that have now become known as ghost hunting tools, although, at bare minimum, all you need is yourself and a flashlight. In Bev's investigations around Maryland, she doesn't even need that because of her sensitivity to the paranormal, but she will bring devices to capture data and recordings. Types of equipment include EMF (electromagnetic field) meters, Infrared thermometers, Infrared motion detectors, dowsing rods, and audiocassette recorders to capture EVPs (electronic voice phenomenon). The type of camera that should be brought along is debated in many circles. Digital cameras have become popular, but many cause the captured image to become pixilated, so a number of ghost hunters will still bring along a 35mm camera.

According to Troy Taylor, founder of the American Ghost Society, in his book, *The Ghost Hunter's Guidebook*, a basic ghost investigation kit should include the following:

- ❀ Notebook and pen
- ❀ Sketch pad and drawing pencils
- ❀ Measuring tape
- ❀ Extra batteries
- ❀ Flashlight
- ❀ Recording device of some kind
- ❀ Small tool kit
- ❀ Camera
- ❀ Video camera
- ❀ Portable motion detectors

All of the devices mentioned above are meant to be used as aids and are not always necessary or conclusive. Lorrie, who is also a sensitive and empathic (terms describing how she's able to feel things around her), had a case in which she and fellow Ghost Chick, Tara, could actually follow an apparition without an EMF detector, which I might point out was not invented to detect ghosts. "We just happened to be in the right place at the right time. We used very little equipment that day!" she said.

Interaction with a ghost or spirit is what ghost hunters are generally looking for, but it may not happen even at locations that have been deemed absolutely positive for paranormal activity. It certainly helps, however, if the ghost hunter begins talking a little bit to the ghosts upon entering, just as if he or she were talking to a normal person. Introductions are generally customary, letting the spirit know that this visit is a friendly one and no harm is intended.

This is a method that Bev Litsinger customarily uses, making sure the atmosphere is relaxed prior to finding out if the spirit is willing to talk to her. If the spirit is willing to interact with her on a friendly level, Bev will begin audio recording and taking a few photographs. There are a number of rather interesting spectral images she's uploaded as slide shows to the Maryland Ghost and Spirit Association website.

Ghosts on film is something everyone — the skeptic, the curious, and the enthusiast — wants to see. Hoax photographs and videos of ghosts are plentiful and the ones that may be legitimate are subject to enormous amounts of scrutiny. Take some time and look up the "Brown Lady of Raynham Hall," the "Lord Combermere Photograph," the "Specter of Newby Church," and the "Tulip Staircase." These are rather famous pictures that each contain an apparition that cannot be explained away as a photographic error or a hoax, yet there are still many people who doubt their authenticity. Anyone trying to photograph the spiritual world will be met with this skepticism.

To help avoid accusations of fraud, there are some photography precautions that should be taken. First of all, make sure that you don't have anything like a finger or even hair protruding in front of the lens. Take care of the lens and make sure it's clean before starting to shoot. My first set of photographs of the Surratt House had a nice yellow-white "orb" floating through each picture. I discovered a speck of something on the lens in time to take another set. Photographs should also not be taken in the rain or snow since bright glows can be created from water droplets. Weather conditions that would cause the lens to fog should also be avoided. The ghost photographer should also be wary of reflective surfaces, mirrors, and bright polished surfaces from which light can reflect back to the camera and give the illusion of spiritual presences.

Ghost hunters should explain to witnesses — those who are considered the host of the location under investigation — what the purpose of the equipment and photography is for. It's already a bit of an intrusion being there, so making them feel comfortable is important. Blending into the background of the location instead of making a spectacle of the investigation makes for a much better experience for everyone.

When the witnesses are comfortable, it is much easier to talk to them and get their version of the circumstances. Interviewing and note-taking is a much bigger part of a ghost investigation than many people realize. From these interviews and the notes that are taken during the investigation, a final report of the findings will be generated.

The actual ghost watch and examining the location of the activity is beyond the scope of this book. There are many books and resources available that provide insight into specific techniques of ghost hunting, what to do when activity is spotted, and how to handle unusual situations.

Ghost hunting is not for the faint of heart. While the practice is becoming more popular, it still involves visiting and possibly interacting with ghosts and spirits that haven't moved on from this world for any number of suspected reasons. While not common, some may not be friendly and try to harm even the expert hunter. If this is something you seriously wish to pursue, do some research, get informed, and possibly take some classes, and find a responsible group with which to go.

13

Haunted Atlas of Maryland

This guide is divided into counties and also includes a small section on Baltimore. Each county section contains a select number of ghost stories and hauntings with each respective location marked on the corresponding county map.

Should you use the information here to plan out your next ghost hunting excursion, please keep in mind that many of these locations are private property and permission to visit will be needed. There are over one hundred locations listed!

Allegeny County

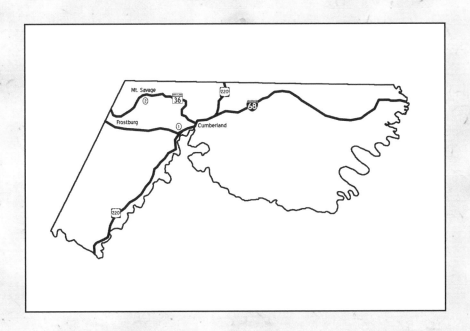

1. Braddock's Gold

During the French and Indian War, British Major General Edward Braddock was marching toward Fort Duquesne, near what is now Pittsburgh, to battle the French, but was ill-prepared for the journey. There were few roads in those days and his troops had to deal with inhospitable terrain, wild animals, insect swarms, and Indian ambushes. It was during these ambushes that Braddock would have gold he was carrying buried for protection. General Braddock never quite made it to Ft. Duquesne; he died from wounds suffered at the Battle of Monongahela. General George Washington carried him away so his body wouldn't be desecrated. While sightings of General Braddock have been reported near his grave, there have also been reports of his spirit traversing the mountains of Allegheny County in search of the gold he left on his march.

Experts say the best places to start looking for his gold—*and his spirit*—are near the many historical markers that dot the path of his march.

2. The Curse of Old Coombs Farm

Local legend has it that a little girl was once sent to buy meat from Old Coombs Farm near Mt. Savage when she stopped to pick an apple from the farm's orchard. Having been told that strangers were not to pick apples from the trees, one of the slaves set a dog after her and she was killed. Angry and grief-stricken, the girl's mother placed a curse upon the family of the farm that each head of the farm for the next one hundred years would die a gruesome death. Seven of the family members suddenly died, five of them violently.

Anne Arundel County

1. Crain House

This once beautiful farmhouse off the Crain Highway became a derelict relic, abandoned and in disrepair, and was then torn down in 2003 even though it had been listed as a Maryland Historic Property. During its time as a haunted house, the old woman who had once owned it had been spotted many times looking out through the upstairs window. Periodically, the kitchen light would be illuminated in the house even though the home had absolutely no power. Police had even once found a dead body in the basement. Also known as the Smith Stoll

House, all that remained after demolition was a solitary grave in the back of the lot that belongs to Sarah Smith, who died in 1865.

2. Eden's Ghostly Procession

Sir Robert Eden was the last English governor of Maryland to have served under King George; he abandoned his property and possessions just before the signing of the Declaration of Independence in 1776. In 1784, he returned to Annapolis and lived out his final days uneventfully. However, when he died shortly thereafter, friends feared that patriots would attempt to desecrate the corpse. His body was carried down Shipwright Street to the water's edge where it was transported and later buried quietly under moonlight at St. Margaret's Churchyard outside of the city. In 1926, the governor's remains were exhumed and returned to Annapolis at St. Anne's Cemetery. Many claim that on dark, foggy nights a ghostly procession carrying Eden's coffin can be seen trekking down Shipwright Street toward the water.

3. The Maryland State House

Thomas Dance was a craftsman working on the dome of the Maryland State House on February 23, 1793, when he slipped and fell from the scaffolding to his death. His family was shipped back to England and was denied the compensation from Dance's work. Since that time, many odd occurrences have been reported at the State House. Disembodied footsteps can be heard at night and many have experienced sudden temperature changes and "cold spots." One time a visitor dismissed the craftsmanship of the dome as unimpressive and a bitter wind suddenly blew open the doors and rattled the chandelier. No one could explain the chill of the gust in the middle of July. On other occasions a man dressed in colonial wear has been spotted walking around the outer ledge of the dome. Many say this is Thomas Dance, upset at the way his family was treated after his death.

4. Loews Annapolis Hotel

The site of the Loews Annapolis Hotel was once the Washington/Baltimore & Annapolis Power Sub-Station, which provided power to the city of Annapolis and the railroad in 1910. The building was purchased by the Annapolis Dairy in 1929 and was used by them for thirty years. In 1991, the building reopened as the Loews Annapolis Hotel and has experienced a number of strange events ever since.

While cleaning up after a banquet, staff heard a loud crash from the third floor service area. As they rushed to the area, the lights began to flicker, but what they discovered was even more puzzling. No milk had been served at the banquet, yet a broken bottle of it was spread all over the floor. What's more, the bottle itself was one that was extraordinarily out-of-date.

In another incident, a waiter cleaning up after-hours experienced the flickering lights, but this time the flickering was followed by a rumble — as if an engine had been started — and the whole room began to vibrate. A bright light shot through the edges of the door to the service corridor, but when he approached the door everything immediately stopped. He was later told of the train that used to run by the power station at 11 p.m. ... the same time of night that he'd had his experience.

Baltimore City

1. Edgar Allan Poe

Long after his death in 1849, Edgar Allan Poe still enthralls the citizens of Baltimore from the annual Poe Festival, to the documents and memorabilia at the Poe Society, to the Poe Room and collection at the Enoch Pratt Free Library, to the tours at the Poe House. One of the most intriguing tributes to the infamous writer takes the form of the "Poe Toaster," a mysterious figure that has visited the Poe grave every year since one hundred years after the author's puzzling death. During the early hours of January 19, the day of Poe's birth, a cloaked figure dressed in black, save for a white scarf, creeps into the Westminster Hall Burial Grounds and leaves three red roses and an unfinished bottle of cognac at Poe's grave. It's suspected that the three red roses are for the three bodies resting in the plot: Poe, his wife, Virginia Clemm Poe, and his mother-in-law, Maria Clemm. Who the Toaster is no one knows for sure, but now that the ritual has reached sixty years, many believe that the original Toaster has passed on the tradition to a younger protégé. The real haunting connected with Edgar Allan Poe, however, is at the house that served as his residence in Baltimore for a period of time during the 1830s at 203 Amity Street (then No. 3 Amity). It is said a rather large woman, quite possibly Poe's grandmother, haunts the house. Doors have been known to open and close by themselves, and visitors have been tapped on the back, but turn around to find no one.

2. Fells Point

Originally a waterfront community in the early 1700s featuring shipbuilding yards, bars, and boarding houses, Fells Point is now a popular tourist attraction with a thriving nightlife. It seems, however, that many of the original inhabitants are enjoying the attention. Featured in the History Channel documentary *Haunted Baltimore*, the Whistling Oyster has had its fill of disembodied footsteps. Plus there was an ash bucket that would continually appear in the aisle near the fireplace even after it was moved elsewhere and the apparition of a slave near the fireplace sweeping the floor. Shakespeare Street has a classy apparition: a man dressed in fine, dated clothing strolling west suddenly disappears. Other apparitions throughout the Fells Point area include a little girl skipping and a fisherman in overalls and smoking a pipe in Bertha's Bar, a man in hat and cloak in a dance studio, and the periodic colonial soldier marching down the street.

The famous burial marker of Edgar Allan Poe, his wife, and his mother-in-law (who was also his aunt).

3. Ft. McHenry

Best known on a national level as the birthplace of "The Star Spangled Banner" penned by Francis Scott Key during the War of 1812, Ft. McHenry is better known around the local Baltimore vicinity for its many haunts. Originally built in 1776 for the American Revolution, Ft. McHenry also saw action during the Civil War, keeping its guns pointed toward Baltimore in order to prevent the city from falling into the hands of southern sympathizers. Many believe they have seen the ghost of Lieutenant Levi Clagett, an officer killed during the British bombardment on September 13, 1814, walking along the ramparts where his fate was sealed.

One of the interior buildings has also seen its fair share of haunts, including a figure in white walking along the second floor, an artist being struck in the head as if "with a frying pan," and a park ranger being pushed down the stairs by a woman dressed in early nineteenth century garb. There's also the sad story of Private John Drew, a distraught soldier who took his life after being locked up for falling asleep on guard duty. Many have felt an eerie chill in his cell and have seen the apparition of a young soldier patrolling the battery where Drew had been assigned in 1880.

4. Garrett-Jacobs Mansion

This grand mansion was built by Robert Garrett, the president of the B & O Railroad in 1884, but took on the name Jacobs when his wife married Henry Barton Jacobs following Robert's death in 1896. After the Jacobs' passed on, the Engineer's Club took control of the building in 1961 and have felt the presence of others ever since. Shadowy figures as well as a full table of ghostly guests raising their glasses in the dining room have been seen in the mansion, but the most notorious sighting at this home probably involves a former handyman. During one holiday season, Peter Weston, the former food and beverage director, moved a heavy sculpture for the Women's Auxiliary, but the next morning it was back in its original place. Upset, Weston asked Manny, the handyman, about the sculpture, but Manny denied knowing anything about it. The handyman turned in his resignation on Christmas Eve; his final working day was to be New Year's Eve, but he suddenly took ill and died that December 31. Nearly a month later, Weston was working downstairs and saw Manny sitting in a chair by the bar where he normally took his break. Instinctively, Weston said, "Hello Manny," but when he turned back, shocked, Manny had vanished.

5. Locust Point Home

This private home near Ft. McHenry has had reports of ghostly activity for more than 150 years. Not long after the Civil War ended, neighbors began telling stories of the house being haunted by the ghost of an old Englishwoman who had starved to death with her children at the home. As the tale goes, her husband had run off and left her with nothing, and she bore too much pride to ask for help. She was found in a rocking chair near a window with the two little ones in her lap. Since then, neighbors claim to sometimes see her rocking back and forth in the window. When the Boidie family moved in during 1865, they immediately had problems with crying echoing throughout the house at night and the creaking of a rocking chair upstairs when there was no rocking chair in the house whatsoever. The ghost also took to slapping members of the family and they soon moved out.

6. Loyola College's McAuley Hall

McAuley Hall has had a few sightings of a young man appearing and disappearing in a dorm room. Doors have periodically closed—forcefully—by themselves and objects will sometimes inexplicably fall from secured locations.

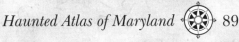

7. Madison Avenue Grounds

A lost ballpark from Baltimore's past, the Madison Avenue Grounds served as the home of the local Pastimes and Maryland ball clubs from 1860 to 1875. The 1869 Sachse *Bird's Eye View of Baltimore* includes a sketch of the relic, but no photographs can be found. The type of baseball played there was before masks and gloves were used, football-type scores were put up (in 1867 the Pastimes beat the New York Mutuals there 47-31), and hard hit groundballs were called "daisy cutters." The only reminder of the baseball grounds from that time is a park at the end of Linden Avenue that had once served as a skating pond. Another nearby reminder of Baltimore's history is the remnant of the old streetcar system that still exists on Linden Avenue. Baseball moved on to Newington Park with Eutaw Place extended through the outfield. Madison Avenue Grounds became a distant memory as row houses were built overtop, but on a casual stroll along the boulevard on Eutaw Place, one can sometimes hear the echo of the smack of a bat against a single-seamed leather ball.

8. The O'Donnell Heights Phantom

For several weeks in the summer of 1951, residents of the O'Donnell Heights neighborhood insisted that a strange "phantom" was lurking in the streets and leaping tall fences. Witnesses stated the being wore a black robe and was only seen at night, prompting the residents of O'Donnell Heights to wait in groups on porches with weapons late at night. The situation was dire enough that the *Baltimore Sun* actually featured an article about it. One man stated that the phantom, dressed completely in black, jumped off a roof and was chased into a graveyard. Mount Carmel Cemetery, Oheb Shalom Cemetery, and St. Stanislaus Cemetery engulf the neighborhood and the phantom could have leapt into any one of these. The panic reached a point in which police were arresting scores of teenagers loitering in graveyards, hoping to capture the phantom and, in the process, make the news. However, the adventures of the O'Donnell Heights Phantom ended there in 1951; the mysterious black-clad figure has not been seen again.

D. USS Constellation

The last sailing warship built by the United States Navy, the *USS Constellation* now rests in Baltimore's Inner Harbor after serving in the Civil War and then for training and ceremonial purposes in Annapolis at the United States Naval Academy. The oddity about the ghost stories with the *USS Constellation* is that their origins predominantly center around the first *USS Constellation* built in 1797 and not the one currently residing in Baltimore, which was built in 1855. During a battle with the French ship *La Vengeance* in 1799, Neil Harvey ran from his post and was sentenced to death. The manner of his capital punishment has ranged from sword, to lynching, to being blown apart by a cannon, but many contend that they have seen the full-bodied apparition of Neil Harvey floating along the decks of the current ship. In 1964, a Catholic priest believed he had received a guided tour by one of the staff members dressed as Captain Thomas Truxtun, the original *Constellation's* legendary leader. After breaking with the guide, the priest complimented one of the other staff on the outstanding presentation he'd just seen, but the staff member stated they had no one of that description working on board and a search of the vessel revealed no one else. A small boy working on the ship as a powder monkey in the 1820s was said the have died below deck, and his ghost has reportedly been seen on board from time to time. One paranormal report dates all the way back to 1863, in which Moses Stafford, lawyer and ranking staff petty officer, made note that Ike Simmons, the cook's mate, saw two recently deceased seamen dancing and singing before him.

Also in the Westminster Hall Burial Grounds is a marker for Edgar Allan Poe's original burial plot. Poe's grandfather is buried nearby as well

10. Westminster Hall

The Westminster Hall Burial Grounds is the resting place for more than just Edgar Allan Poe. The grounds also contains the bodies of General Samuel Smith, who helped organize the defense of Baltimore during the War of 1812; Colonel James McHenry, for whom Fort McHenry was named; five former mayors of Baltimore; and fourteen other generals who had served during the American Revolution and the War of 1812. The church was built over a pre-existing cemetery and much of the former graveyard can only be reached via the catacombs underneath the building. Quite a number of visitors to the catacombs have heard strange whispers and felt the soft touch of unseen hands as they walk through. Unexplained cold spots have been reported throughout the burial site as well.

11. Zodiac Restaurant & Club Charles

— *See Chapter Eleven*

Baltimore County

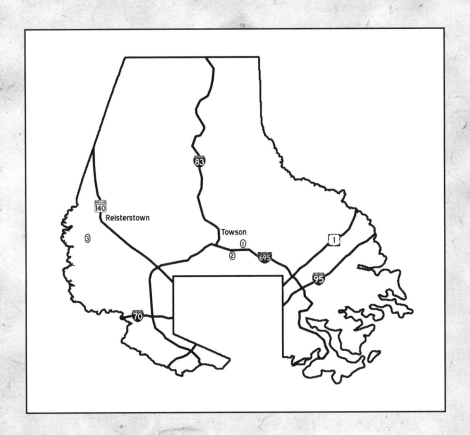

1. Hampton Mansion

Nicknamed "Ridgley's Folly" by the surrounding country-folk, Hampton Mansion was built by Captain Charles Ridgely between 1783 and 1790, a gorgeous aristocratic home with lavish rooms set in the style of ancient Rome and Greece. The house is so beautiful that a former butler has stayed on to occasionally greet guests at the door...even after his life ended.

Other spectral visitors include Cygnet, the daughter of a former governor who has been seen combing her hair, and the former owner Charles Ridgely... the latter returned to the mansion in a stagecoach hours after he died. Another famous Hampton haunting is the sound of the great chandelier crashing and emanating throughout the house, but the chandelier has always remained intact and attached to the ceiling.

2. Old Medix School

While the site of the Old Medix School in Towson may now be commercial property, its ghosts may still remain. The former school was once a hotel and brought with it a ghost from its past. Believing the CIA was chasing him, a man killed himself on the third floor of the hotel. The room in which he died eventually became the teacher's lounge...and a number of times the cabinets would open and close on their own, disembodied footsteps could be heard, and the ghost would sometimes turn the doorknob. There were also times the elevator would oddly run on its own accord.

3. Soldier's Delight

Soldier's Delight is a natural serpentine barren where chrome was first discovered in the United States. For a time in the 1800s, Isaac Tyson, Jr. operated chromite mines from this location and other barrens, producing nearly all the world's supply of chromium. Now a natural preserve, it had once been an Indian hunting ground and had also been the site of a few minor skirmishes between the Union Army and the Maryland Volunteers of the Confederate Army during the Civil War. Local legends of the park include a Confederate soldier buried in an old graveyard and a witch hanged in the woods by the frightened citizens of Reisterstown. Another hanging occurred in the late 1800s when a man murdered his unfaithful wife and was sentenced to death. Berryman's Lane nearby is supposed to be named after him. Hikers trekking along the paths through the woods have heard odd sounds, voices, and have felt an overall creepiness in some areas.

Calvert County

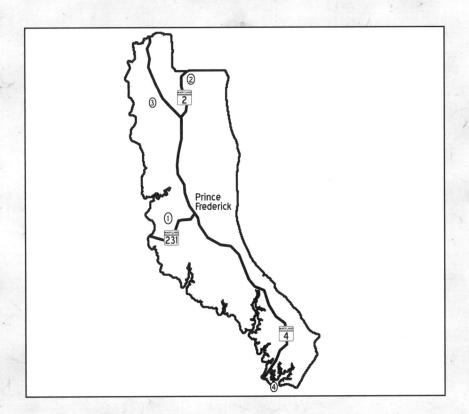

1. Cedar Hill

The Cedar Hill Country Estate was built by John Bigger in the late 1600s and is quite unique in Maryland for its "cross shape" architecture. Now a bed and breakfast, a reception hall for weddings, and a museum, Cedar Hill also shares with us some of its ghosts. Former tenants have been tapped on the shoulder by invisible hands, and a visiting family member once saw a Civil War soldier standing in the living room. A throw rug in the downstairs hall, no matter how many times it was placed out, would be found rolled up in the corner. Odd noises sometimes emanate from the attic and a few people have felt a push down the stairs.

2. The Gray Lady of Maidstone

Maidstone, the most legendary of haunted houses in Calvert County, has been home to the spirit of a beautiful young woman dressed in gray for nearly two hundred years. Most people believe the ghost to be that of Ann Chew, wife of Philip Chew, with whom she resided with at Maidstone in the early 1700s. Her attire has given her the nickname "The Gray Lady." Ann's interactions with the living have generally been courteous, giving the general passerby a nice smile. However, there have also been times when she's been known to push a person or two off the couch in the living room.

3. Northern High School

It is believed that part of Northern High School was built over a slave graveyard that was used by the Old Ward House plantation. Posters have been flung from the walls, objects have shot up into the air, and sometimes eerie moans and the dragging of chains can be heard down the hallways.

4. Solomons Island

Solomons Island isn't very large, but it is littered with a number of ghost stories.

❀ At Bowen's Inn, an employee was carrying boxes up the stairs when he spotted a woman in an old black dress and lace collar...she proceeded to walk down the hall as he ran off.

❀ In 1940, when a man was staying at the old home that is now Carmen's Gallery, he fell off a pier and drowned, but his suitcase had been left behind and was later placed in the attic. Although an apparition of the man has never appeared, strange noises can be heard at times throughout the house.

❀ The Gray Fox Inn is said to be haunted by a small poodle that lived with the family that built the home in 1913. The dog doesn't appear in its entirety, but its back half can usually be seen wagging its tail.

Caroline County

1. Drawbridge Gypsy

The old Denton drawbridge that spanned the Choptank River has a strange tale associated with it. In the late 1800s, a local gypsy was murdered by her seven brothers because they did not want her to marry a certain man. Her fellow gypsies placed a curse on the brothers and every year for seven years one of the brothers fell to his death. Now every August, for nearly the past one hundred years, the two lovers have been seen reunited in the afterlife, riding a ghostly white stallion together near the old drawbridge.

2. Patty Cannon

Patty Cannon, a strong, large woman, was an infamous kidnapper, black marketer, and murderess who lived along the Maryland and Delaware border during the early 1800s. Patty's son-in-law, Joe Johnson, ran a tavern and inn and Patty would murder many of the visitors, stealing their belongings and horses. One account stated that she roasted a live baby in her fireplace because she could no longer put up with the infant's crying. It's suspected that she also killed her husband. Patty also made a profession of illegally selling freedmen as slaves after the slave trade had been abolished in 1808. Legends carry on about how when authorities came to her house in Maryland she would skip over to her barn in Delaware and mock them and vise-versa. She was finally arrested by Delaware authorities in 1829 and committed suicide while awaiting trial. Patty's body was placed in a pauper's field behind the courthouse until the early 1900s. During an enlargement of the courthouse, a young boy stole the skull of Patty Cannon when the remains from the pauper's field were being moved to another site. The boy made a showcase of the skull in his barn and charged visitors twenty-five cents to give it a rub for luck. Today, the skull is in the care of the Dover, Delaware, Library and is available for anyone to see. The old tavern in Reliance, Maryland, was open for a time as a museum. Visitors often talked of feeling an evil presence about the house while doors slammed shut and disembodied footsteps could be heard. The owner at the time eventually vacated the premises, stating he could no longer deal with all the hauntings. The original "Patty Cannon House" was demolished in 1948, with a newer version erected nearby.

Carroll County

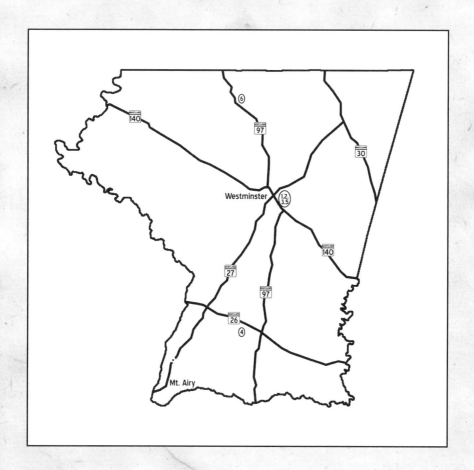

1. Cockey's Tavern

2. The Fiery Furnace

3. Headless Tom

— *See Chapter Four*

4. Living Faith Farm

Also known as Leppo Farm, the house was built in 1827 for the Church of the Brethren. There have been a variety of different antics carried on by the spirits here.

❀ One of the ghosts seems to be that of a child. Scribbles in crayon have appeared on the ceiling and sometimes the sound of a child's ball being dropped can be heard on the steps. The words "my love" have been written in a child's penmanship a number of times on a window screen.

❀ There's an interesting reaction from animals as dogs have bolted from rooms with wicker baskets being thrown at them, and cats have laid down, purring as if they were being petted.

❀ At a Christmas celebration one year a candle was lifted out of its holder, floated through the air about six feet, extinguished, and then dropped to the floor.

❀ Also, at an adjacent antique shop, a Civil War soldier has been spotted rocking in the front porch chair.

5. Opera House Ghost

— *See Chapter Four*

6. Silver Run Mine

Small copper and gold mines have opened and closed over the years in Carroll County, but none more famous than the only silver mine ever heard of in Maryland. In the 1780s, near the town of Silver Run, a German silversmith created and sold his wares. Locals and travelers alike, including his own daughter, were amazed with the quantity and low price of the silver merchandise he sold. At her constant urging, he finally succumbed to his daughter's wishes to share his secret, so he blindfolded her and guided her into the woods. He led her into a cave on Rattlesnake Hill and, when he removed the blindfold, she was amazed at all the silver she saw before her in his lantern-lit light. He told her that the local Indians had shared with him their secrets because of a friendship they had forged, but the secret could never leave their family lest a curse be placed upon them that only the sacrifice of three lives could break. After mining some of the silver, he blindfolded his daughter again and they set back for home, but his daughter left a trail of small twigs behind. Upon arriving home, she immediately ran and told a friend, and at the friend's urging they followed the trail of twigs back to the cave. Three days later the silversmith and his daughter were dragged out of their beds and taken to the cave where their lives were taken. After a few days, the locals grew suspicious of the silversmith's disappearance and, led by the daughter's friend, set out for the cave of silver. However, the cave had vanished just as quickly as the silversmith and his daughter. For years afterwards, people in the area have claimed to see the specter of a man in a broad-brimmed hat carrying a lantern, sometimes accompanied by a ghostly girl, roaming the hills until three sacrifices are made for their redemption.

Cecil County

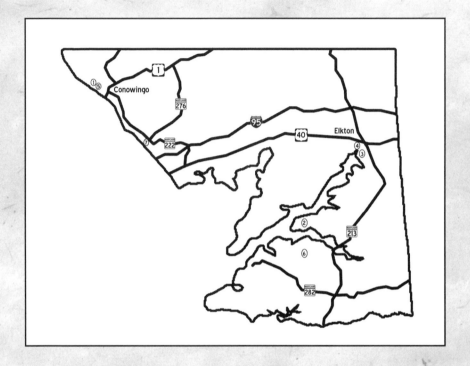

1. Bell Manor

Since the 1970s, Girl Scouts have been using the area around Bell Manor as a campground and there are a couple of ghost stories associated with the antebellum mansion that they have passed down over the years. One is about a woman in a formal green dress who hanged herself from the banister in the late 1800s. Her image is seen from time to time floating in the house. The grounds also include a chimney from the original house that was burned down during the Civil War. Bell Plantation had been a part of the Underground Railroad and soldiers came one dark night to set fire to the home. The woman of the house hid her children in the fireplace, but all perished in the blaze. The cries of the children can still be heard at times emanating from the chimney.

2. Bohemia House Bed and Breakfast

Built in 1850, this house is suspected to have been used as part of the Underground Railroad, hiding and moving slaves through the tunnels and catacombs that run from the basement of the home to the river. One previous owner, Margaret, is believed to have been murdered there and her body stashed in the catacombs. No one knows for sure since she disappeared in 1920 and has never been found. Employees of the bed and breakfast have heard strange organ music and voices throughout the house, and any time they try to use artificial flowers, they are removed from their vases and tossed to the floor. One bedroom is particularly active. A clock on a dresser will move from one side of the furniture to the other, the closet door will open on its own, and many times the bed sheets are thrown to the side with no explanation.

3. Frenchtown Tavern

When the Frenchtown Tavern existed, there were a number of odd incidents that happened within its walls.

✸ Workers spending the night one evening couldn't sleep from the repeated sounds of footsteps and chains.

✸ A ghostly hand once appeared on the stairwell and yanked an unsuspecting girl down the stairs by the ankle.

✸ A crucifix was pulled off of a wall in the bedroom and thrown across the room.

✸ There were also sightings of a uniformed man, most likely a Civil War soldier, who was known as "the gray man."

While the site of the Frenchtown Tavern still exists, the house burned to the ground in the 1960s as a result of children playing with fire.

4. Indian Chief of Elk Creek

In the early 1980s the Cecil County government decided to build a detention center near the location where Little Elk Creek and Big Elk Creek met. Before construction began, archaeologists investigated the site for historical artifacts and discovered the location had been an Indian village, dating back to at least 1400. They found numerous pottery shards, arrowheads, and gravesites, but once the research had been completed and documented, construction began on the detention center. Before the prison even opened, there were reports from the nightshift workers that strange footsteps could be heard and lights would arbitrarily go on and off. However, the strangest tale came just after the detention center opened its doors. One of the bigger prisoners spent most of one frightful night pinned to his bed by what appeared to be an Indian chief, complete with war paint and a full bonnet of feathers. The two didn't talk to each other, but struggled throughout the night and into the next morning as the Indian apparition continued to press down against the inmate. The prisoner refused to sleep in the cell again and began sharing one with another prisoner.

5. The Red Light

During the Civil War, a family of slaves had taken flight on a raft up the Susquehanna River, working together to fight the current. They'd been told that a red light would mark a safe landing place for them and shelter and food would be provided until they made it to a safe house. Unfortunately, slave hunters had gotten word of the rendezvous, ambushed the waiting camp at the red light, and were ready for the slaves when the raft arrived. It's not certain what happened; some say the slaves put up a fight and were killed while others claim the slaves were captured and sold. The answer may lie in the ghostly activity along the Susquehanna just north of the Conowingo Dam. Fishermen and hikers have told stories of a ghostly red light along the shore and moans of the slaves from the raft on the river. Some think the dead of that night are telling their story as spectral floating corpses, which can be seen in the fog over the water just before dawn.

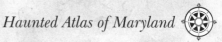

6. Screaming Polly

The legend of Screaming Polly in southern Cecil County has many variations. Most paint her as a servant having died in some sort of snowstorm, but from there the stories change. One states that she was the lover of a wealthy local landowner, but when she became pregnant he banished her from his property. Locals feared the landowner and refused to help Polly, and she died in a blizzard screaming for help. Her cries are still heard to this day when a snowstorm hits the area. Another story claims that the landowner's son fell in love with Polly and the couple planned to elope. The father caught wind of the plan and arranged for the young man to be delayed on his way to meeting the servant girl. There are three variations to the outcome. When the son finally arrived, he discovered Polly dead on the road, run down by a carriage. Or she fled the area to live a life alone, with or without child. Or she never made it to the rendezvous point because she'd been tied to a tree and died during a blizzard. Some locals claim you can only see Polly on October 30–31, along Stemmers Run Road. There a fog will roll in from both sides of the road accompanied with a high-pitch scream. A ghostly white form resembling a young woman will cross the road holding her own head under her left arm. Others have also seen the image of Polly floating along the surface of the Bohemia River.

7. Tome School

Named for Jacob Tome, Cecil County's first millionaire, the Tome School for Boys was considered one of the most majestic boarding schools along the East Coast during the 1920s. During the Second World War in 1942, it was incorporated into the Bainbridge Naval Training Center until it was closed in 1976. It lay dormant for years until, in 1999, Port Deposit finally annexed the school. Not long after Tome School's opening in 1894, a small pox epidemic hit the school, killing a number of the students. While in the hands of the Navy, many working there heard disembodied footsteps and saw the apparitions of children who would disappear when approached.

Charles County

1. The Ghostly Blue Dog

The legend of the blue dog ghost of Port Tobacco dates back to 1658, and, according to a 1962 *Baltimore American* interview with the director of the State Department of Economic Development, George W. Hubley, Jr., Port Tobacco is the oldest ghost town in the United States. On a cold, dark night when the village was a seaport and a hub for shipbuilding, the dog's master stumbled into Port Tobacco as a simple peddler. After a few drinks in a local tavern, the peddler began bragging about the gold he was carrying. The patrons of the tavern didn't believe him, so he showed off the gold and excited the crowd. When he wobbled out of the bar and up Rose Hill Road later that night, he was murdered, as was the dog that faithfully tried to protect its master. The gold was hidden along the roadside and when the attacker came to retrieve it...the blue dog ghost scared him off. Another version of the story replaces the peddler with a soldier who was attacked for his gold and the deed to his estate. Locals claim that every February the ghost of the dog can be seen still protecting the gold.

2. Dr. Samuel A. Mudd House

— *See Chapter Ten*

Dorchester County

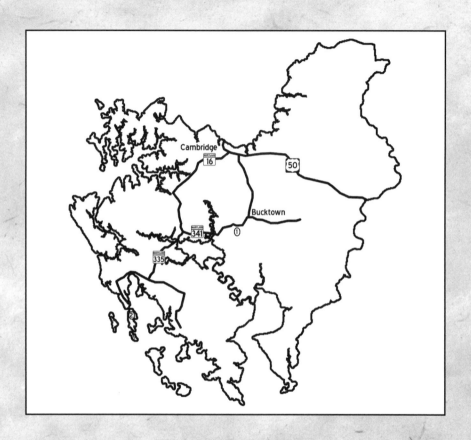

1. Bigg Lizz

Bigg Lizz was such a large woman that her name has been respectfully spelled with double letters. She worked as a slave for a wealthy plantation owner along Maryland's Eastern Shore, but also served as a spy for the Union. Her master found out and devised a plan of how to deal with her when he finished filling a trunk with a secret cache of gold. One humid summer night, he and Bigg Lizz loaded up a wagon with the chest and carted it into the murky Greenbriar Swamp. When they reached a suitable spot, he handed Bigg Lizz a shovel and she dug a large hole that surpassed even her own height. She lowered the chest into the hole and began filling it back up with earth. Standing above her on the wagon, the master wielded a large tobacco knife and sliced off her head, which thudded against a nearby tree, and her large body collapsed over the chest. He buried her with the chest of gold and went back home to sleep. At some point he realized that he had forgotten to retrieve her head, but knowing that in the dark he'd have an impossible time finding it anyway, he left it for animals to eat. At around 3:15 a.m., he awoke to a scratching sound emanating from the corner of the room. He also noticed a bitter chill had swept over his bedchambers, an oddity for the humid summer. He rose from his bed to shut the window when he was confronted by the form of Bigg Lizz, decapitated, clutching her gruesome head with glowing red eyes in one hand and the tobacco knife in the other. Terrified, the master jumped from the window to his death three stories below. It is said that the specter of Bigg Lizz still roams the swamp protecting the treasure for which her earthly body perished. The legend attracts treasure hunters even to this day.

2. The Floating Coffin

Like many other islands, the dead of Hooper Island were generally placed in graves above the ground. During the Great Storm of 1933, a local was trapped in his house from the swelling water when he suddenly heard a tapping noise against a second floor window. He waded over to the window, but since it was dark, he couldn't see what was hitting it. He opened the window and in floated a coffin. In the dim light he recognized the coffin as his recently deceased wife's. Some say he climbed in with her while others say he simply climbed atop; in either case he rode the coffin to safety, declaring when he arrived, "Thanks, old woman! You always did look after me."

Frederick County

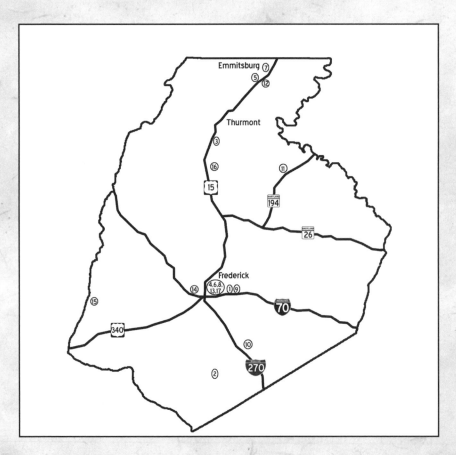

1. A. B. Nebb

An old two-story house became the new home of a young couple and their children in 1970. Not long after they moved in, many strange occurrences started happening. Voices and moans issued forth from empty rooms of the house, footsteps thudded on the stairs, and crashes rang out everywhere. One night, after checking a disturbance in the children's room, the young wife heard a noise at the end of the hall from the area of the bathroom. Although the door had been closed and the light turned off, when she entered the room and turned on the light she discovered a man with curly, brown hair and dirty work boots standing before her. In a stern voice, he said, "Stop the digging! Leave my family alone." Just as soon as he'd said it, he disappeared.

Baffled at what to do, she convinced a neighbor friend to work an Ouija board with her. They were shocked when it started moving, but the information they were given proved to be useful. They were told the spirit was that of A. B. Nebb, who had once lived behind the house in a shack. His wife and child caught ill one year and died. He buried them nearby and visited their graves every day until his own death and beyond. The young woman realized that the digging the ghost referred to might have been the gardening they'd been doing in the back yard. Suspecting that may have been the site of the graves (and not wanting to find out), she and her husband moved their gardening elsewhere and the haunting substantially stopped.

2. Amelung Estates

Frederick Amelung emigrated from Bremen, Germany, with a number of skilled workers in 1784, established New Bremen along Bennett's Creek near the Monocacy, and built the American Glass Manufactory. Very little remains of the site today, and for a time historians were challenged to find records of the village, but it's known that Amelung Estates in the southern part of Frederick County near Park Mills is built over it. An archaeological dig was conducted during the early 1960s and much was discovered about the site, but they failed to find the rumored cemetery. A few years later, a stray dog ambled into the neighborhood with a bone unearthed from a nearby pile of dirt. When two human skulls were also found at this location, it was excavated, revealing the graves of a man in his mid thirties and a small boy around the age of five or six. Although the New Bremen graveyard had been found, other forces were stirred up as well. Residents are now awoken at night to the sounds of children screaming or playing with their toys.

However, when children are checked upon, they're fast asleep. One parent got fed up about the repeated extinguishing of the bathroom nightlight that she woke her daughter and insisted that she stop. The child repeatedly denied turning off the light and then asked to be moved from the room because she kept getting pushed out of bed.

3. Auburn Mansion

This colonial mansion near Catoctin Furnace was built by Baker Johnson in 1808 and was later occupied by the McPherson family for over one hundred years. Twenty year-old Edward McPherson took his brother's place in the war against Mexico in the 1840s and served under General Winfield Scott. Unfortunately, Edward died in a duel with a Lieutenant Maddox on March 16, 1847, and his body was sent home in a barrel of whiskey. Edward's ghost now roams the halls of Auburn mansion, a rather friendly ghost who opens doors for guests and has become known as "Sir" Edward.

4. Barbara Fritchie House

— *See Chapter Five*

5. The Christmas Flute

Larry Dielman was the son of renowned musician Casper Dielman who came to America from Germany in the 1800s. Casper directed orchestras in New York, Philadelphia, and Baltimore, and composed inaugural music for four presidents before settling down as a Professor at Mount Saint Mary's College in 1834. Larry was not quite as talented as his father, but would often play at his father's side and would use his talents to try to charm women. When his father died, Larry paid tribute to him by playing a flute at his gravestone, near Grotto of Our Lady of Lourdes, the following Christmas. Upon hearing the music, many of the townspeople walked up the hill and paid their respects. This became a tradition each year after, and when Larry became too old to trudge up the snowy hill, townsfolk would pull him up by sled. Even after Larry's death, the sound of his flute could still faintly be heard in the air every Christmas.

6. Gaslight Antiques

— *See Chapter Five*

7. Haunted Training

The site of FEMA's Emergency Management Institute in Emmitsburg was once the site of a hospital used during the Civil War where many soldiers were treated after the battle of Gettysburg. Students staying there for training have reported a number of odd incidents including the television in one's room repeatedly turning on and off and one student seeing the face of a man in the mirror while he was shaving. The ghostly image of a nun has been seeing floating past the freezers in the dining facility and the security guards are reluctant to make their rounds in the basement of the chapel, which had served as a morgue during the war.

8. Historical Society of Frederick County

— *See Chapter Five*

9. Jug Monument

In 1808, Leonard Harbaugh was credited with building what became known as the "Jug Bridge" for the National Road. Spanning the Monocacy River, he marked his creation with a large demijohn, or a jug-shaped object, on the eastern side of the bridge. General Marquis de Lafayette crossed it in 1824 during a final victory tour of the Revolutionary War, and nearby thanked a delegation for the warm greeting he'd received. In 1942, 134 years after it had been built, the Jug Bridge partially collapsed and a new one was built alongside, with the jug moved to a small park. A legend has been maintained for two

What are the strange noises heard around the Jug Monument? Are they related to a possible hidden whiskey bottle inside the demijohn?

hundred years that Harbaugh placed a real bottle of whiskey inside the demijohn. It's also been said that Civil War soldiers also used the jug to hide their whiskey. Those passing by prior to the move said they heard strange noises radiating from the jug—and it's been said those noises have followed the jug to its new location. Some believe those old Civil War soldiers may still be searching for that bottle of whiskey they somehow hid in or around the jug.

10. Landon

The Landon mansion was originally built in Virginia around 1754, but was then disassembled and moved to Urbana, Maryland, in 1846. It served a short-term role as the Shirley Academy for Women just before the Civil War and then was used as a convalescent home during the war. Confederate General J. E. B. Stuart used the house as his headquarters for a brief time and is known to have hosted his Sabers and Roses Ball there just before the Battle of Antietam. The apparition of a woman dressed in white and wearing a shawl is known to try to tuck in children on the second floor. Some think she's from the Shirley Academy days while others think she may be the wife of Colonel Luke Tiernan Brien, Stuart's chief of staff who bought 180 acres of land around Landon after the war. It's believed it is his spirit that has been seen walking around the basement. Ghost dogs that died in the early 1900s when then owner kept a pack of them in the basement have been heard on the premises as well when no other dogs were around.

11. Miss Molly

In the quiet town of Woodsboro is a Victorian home that is the residence of the spirit known as "Miss Molly." Molly is known to sing in the kitchen and periodically open a door, but on rare occasions, her hauntings can become a little less subtle. Sometimes she will sit on the edge of a bed, a weight will push it down, and an impression will be left. At other times, she will try to make an appearance in the ghostly shape of her earthly form. It's believed her spirit remained there to torment her cruel father, which drove him insane and caused him to hang himself from a tree in the backyard. Now she's left to haunt whomever may live there.

12. Mount St. Mary's College

Its proximity to Gettysburg and the fact that it is the second oldest Catholic university in the country makes Mount St. Mary's prime ground for ghosts and spirits. One of its most famous is that of Reverend Simon Bruté, the first spiritual director of the Seminary. He's been known to roam the campus in flowing black robes and will sometimes get in step behind groups of unsuspecting students, nodding at passersby. A favorite haunt of one ghost is Room 252 in one of the older dormitories on campus. Here, students have experienced lights flickering on and off, the television arbitrarily switching stations, and random flushes of the toilet. A visiting priest staying in the room once reported his belongings being tossed about the room after returning one night. Beds have been known to move with people in them in this room and some have reported the uncanny ability of "knowing" things while there. Also, a morbid Confederate soldier has been known to walk the grounds at night and will sometimes tap people on the shoulder.

13. National Civil War Medicine Museum

— *See Chapter Five*

14. Prospect Hall

Prospect Hall was a colonial mansion built in 1732 by Frederick surveyor Daniel Dulany and is now part of St. John's Catholic School. Dulany's son fell in love with a mulatto slave of which his father would have no part. He sent his son away to England and, according to legend, Daniel boarded up the girl in the walls of the house and allowed her to suffocate there. While later owners claimed to have heard knocking from the walls, the ghost of the girl has been a free and modern spirit in recent years. She become known as "Agnes" around the school and has been seen about the building, particularly in the library and computer center. She seems to be interested in technology and is known to play around with the computers quite often.

15. Spook Hill

Also known as Gravity Hill, the location is debatable, but many contend that the famed location is near Burkittsville along Gapland Road. As the legend goes, if you leave your car in neutral at the bottom of the hill it will begin moving upward on its own. The belief is that Civil War ghosts are pushing the car up the hill as they had once pushed their artillery.

16. Utica Covered Bridge

Near Lewistown is a covered bridge that once spanned the Monocacy River, but was washed away in 1889. The local townsfolk gathered up the remains and rebuilt it over Fishing Creek, and for a time, children used to use this location as a swimming hole. Many years ago, a young boy drowned there and the children stopped using it in fear they would meet the same fate. There have been numerous reports of a glowing apparition climbing out of the water and of spectral cries from the stream. The boy has also been seen on the bridge. A motorist once told the story of how one foggy night on the bridge he saw, for a split second, in front of his car, a boy standing on the bridge dripping wet. He slammed on his brakes and thought he had hit the child, so he leapt out of the car after stopping. He looked underneath, but saw no one there. However, when he turned around he saw the boy behind his car staring at him. Before the man could get a word out of his mouth, the boy's image disappeared into the fog.

17. Weinberg Center for the Performing Arts

— *See Chapter Five*

Garrett County

1. Deep Creek Lake

One Christmas, a man and a number of his friends were riding new snowmobiles out on the frozen lake. There was an unfortunate accident when one of the snowmobiles broke through the ice and three of the men drowned. The wives of one of the men had been decorating the Christmas tree with her daughters when there was a knock on the door. When she answered, her husband was standing before her dripping wet. She tried to grab his arm to rush him inside, but her hand went through his form and then he disappeared. She

thought she was imagining things and closed the door. A few minutes later the sheriff's deputy arrived at the door to deliver the tragic news.

2. Ghost Towns

Logging and mining were thriving industries in northwestern Maryland during the 1800s and into the early 1900s. Progress and the depletion of natural resources eliminated the purpose of the many small towns that had cropped up to house the industries' workers and they have since morphed into ghost towns. Ghost town seekers need only look up names like Bloomington, Deer Park, Dodson, Gorman, Shaw, and Vindex to find some wonderful relics to investigate.

Harford County

1. Currier House Bed and Breakfast

Named for Matthew Currier who moved his family into this historic Havre de Grace home in 1861, the Currier House now serves as a successful bed and breakfast. Although the building was originally constructed in 1790, the same family has resided in it for nearly 150 years and has seen it through many renovations. There is a ghost of an eight-year-old girl that lingers about and calls herself "G. Z." She remains in one room and moves a few objects around, but is relatively friendly. She's been known to shake the hangers in the closet from time to time when someone tries to speak with her. Who she may be and what connection she has to the house is still unknown, although it's possible she may have had something to do with the Underground Railroad, which ran through the house long ago.

2. The Headless Peddler

In the 1700s, peddlers were a common sight on the countryside, trying to sell their wares to anyone who crossed their path. At a gristmill at Rock Run in 1783, the slumped body of a headless peddler was discovered. The miller searched for the head, but none was found and a quick burial was arranged. Soon after, the specter of the headless peddler started appearing in the area on a regular basis poking a stick at the ground. Eighty years later, a farmer was digging a drainage ditch not far from the old mill when he discovered a human skull. There was no body to be found and, with only one story in the area about a decapitation, he deduced it must belong to the peddler. He found the gravesite and reunited the head with the body. Thereafter, the ghost of the peddler was never seen again. It is now believed that the ground-poking activity of the ghost was to show people where the peddler's head was located so it could be paired back with its body.

3. Jericho Covered Bridge

This eighty-foot long covered bridge built in the mid 1800s connects Jericho Road from Baltimore County to Harford County and is close to the 235-year-old Jerusalem Mill. The site has become a lure for ghost hunters who seek the spirits of the tales that have been passed down over the years. Slaves were said to have been hanged from the bridge's rafters as they tried to flee across the Mason Dixon line, although this may be debatable since it can't be confirmed when precisely the bridge was built (some say 1865 while other sources say it may have been built as far back as 1850). Still, people claim to have had their cars stopped on the bridge for no explainable reason, and a woman in 1800s garb has been seen strolling along the roadside.

4. Liriodendron Mansion

Liriodendron Mansion is a beautiful estate that was built in 1898 as a summer home for Johns Hopkins Hospital founder, Dr. Howard Kelly. Today it is used for weddings, meetings, and as a museum, but it is also used by spirits from the past. Guests and staff alike have each heard disembodied footsteps within the old home, although an apparition of whatever haunts the place has yet to be seen.

Howard County

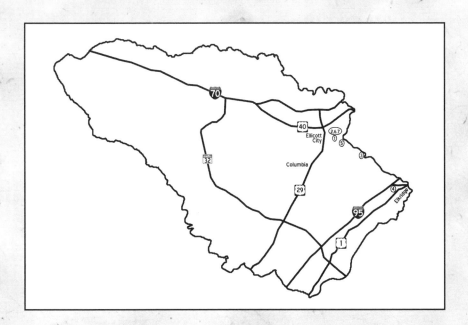

1. Ellicott City Fire Stations

Old firehouses in Ellicott City are one of this historic town's famous haunts.

❁ Built in 1889, Ellicott City's first fire station is now a museum that is opened by appointment only. Slamming doors and the sound of footsteps have been repeatedly heard.

❁ Fire Station 2, built in 1930, is now the Wine Bin, but its non-alcoholic spirits still linger from the old firehouse days. Firefighters who used to work there would blame odd noises on "Mr. Harry," a reference to B. Harrison Shipley, the fire chief who served there from 1935 to 1957.

2. Hayden House

— *See Chapter Seven*

3. Ilchester Hell House

Originally named Mount St. Clemens and then later titled St. Mary's College by a religious order known as the Redemptorists, the school ruins at Ilchester have become a local legend in the area as "Hell House." Although little remains now after a fire forced the dismantling of the rest of the ruins, stories of Hell House still loom large.

After the seminary school closed in the 1970s due to low attendance, local rumor started that the school closed following the murders of students. While this is likely a complete myth, its circulation caused teenagers to venture up the steep slopes of the hill where the building stood and conjure up more tales.

The caretaker, Allen Hudson, developed a reputation as well; with his Rottweilers and shotgun, he'd chase off groups of teens trespassing the grounds looking for a thrill, including one he'd shot in the shoulder when he'd been threatened with baseball bats. Some say they heard strange voices around the grounds and others say they saw apparitions, but it's hard to discern fact from the fiction when some stories included nuns sacrificed in a pentagram.

4. Lawyer's Hill

Lawyer's Hill in Elkridge is the site of many fine homes, but one in particular, The Lawn, has been home to a rather mischievous poltergeist for a number of years. Doors lock and unlock by themselves, food has been known to shoot up in the air, and a key for a grandfather clock would go missing and then reappear out of nowhere. These sorts of things happened with a number of different lockable items including the front door and a cupboard in an upstairs bedroom.

An Ouija board was brought in to try to help determine what was going on and it was indicated that there are more than one spirit haunting the house. One young boy had been seen talking with an invisible party and, when asked what he was doing, he became exasperated and explained how he was conversing with a number of people that used to live at The Lawn.

The bell tower at Lilburn.

5. Lilburn Castle
— *See Chapter Eight*

6. Mount Ida Visitor's Center

7. Patapsco Female Institute
— *See Chapter Six*

Kent County

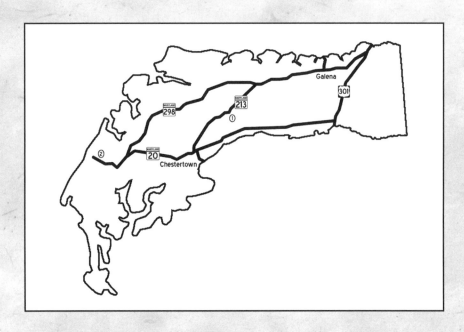

1. The Bleeding Stone of White House Farm

The tale goes that a young girl, an indentured servant, was making to escape White House Farm to run off with her lover. Within minutes in the pale early morning light, her horse fell and she smashed her head against a large rock, killing her. No one can verify her name, but they all recall her story since the rock upon which she bled to death remains cursed. The rock has been painted over many times, but no matter how much it is painted or whitewashed, the bloodstain always rises to the surface.

The house, originally known as Ridgely Estate, also has its own ghosts, including spirits that make noises in upstairs bedrooms and one ghostly woman that appears in a blue nightgown. The ghost of Mary Perkins Stuart is also said to walk the grounds each year. Many claim that she is also the ghost of the young girl and the woman in the blue nightgown, but there is also a large contingent who believe these are three separate ghosts.

2. The Inn at Mitchell House

While many historic houses and manors have been turned into bed and breakfasts with manicured grounds that offer a picturesque setting for weddings, The Inn at Mitchell House near Chestertown has a unique historical aspect that others don't — a British officer died there on the kitchen table during the War of 1812. Critically wounded, Sir Peter Parker was being carried back to his ship when he was brought to the house so his wounds could be tended. He was unable to be saved. His ghost, however, is not likely the one that haunts the house.

One of the bedrooms used to contain a rocking chair, which many guests claimed would rock by itself from time to time. Also, while sitting in it, people would feel something brush past their legs and the family cat refused to enter the room. Of interesting note, shackles for slaves were once bolted to the walls of the basement, but were removed only about ten years before the current owners bought the estate in 1986.

Montgomery County

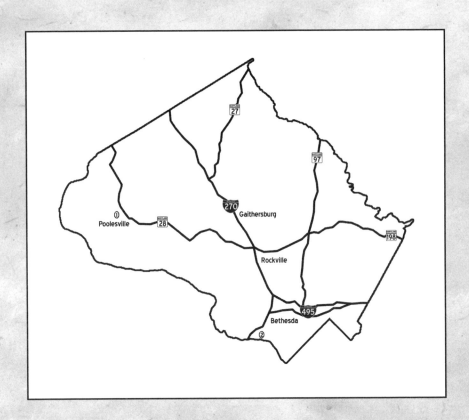

1. Annington Manor

Located in Poolesville, Annington Manor was a strategic lookout for Union troops throughout the Civil War since from its hilltop it had a wonderful view of the Maryland and Virginia countryside. Colonel Robert Baker, a Senator from Oregon, ate his last dinner at Annington before he died the following day at the Battle of Ball's Bluff. His spirit is said to be one that haunts the grounds of Annington. He and other soldiers are buried in a small national cemetery on the property and the estate has taken on the nickname "Haunted House Bend."

2. Clara Barton House

Clara Barton founded the American Red Cross in 1881, and her house in Glen Echo, where she spent the final fifteen years of her life, is now a historic site commemorating her achievements. There have been a few reports that Clara still roams the premises, sometimes described as wearing dark clothing dating back to the late 1800s.

Prince George's County

1. Bladensburg Dueling Grounds

Just outside of the Washington D.C. limits is the Bladensburg dueling grounds where military officers and congressmen used to meet to settle their differences. There were twenty-six duels known to have been fought there, although there may have been more. The most famous duel was between Commodore Stephen Decatur and Commodore James Barron. Each of their first shots hit their mark, but while Barron was only injured, Decatur died from his wounds two days later. While Decatur's spirit is said to visit the grounds from time to time,

Portraits of the Snowdens overlook the library at Montpelier Mansion. Do their ghosts overlook the house as well?

more commonly reported is the spirit of Daniel Key, son of Francis Scott Key. He and friend John Sherborne dueled over an argument about the speed of two steamboats and Key was dead at the young age of twenty.

2. Montpelier Mansion

— *See Chapter Three*

3. Mt. Airy Mansion and Plantation

— *See Chapter Two*

4. Oaklands

— *See Chapter Three*

5. The Surratt House

— *See Chapter Nine*

Queen Anne's County

1. Bloomingdale Mansion

Bloomingdale Mansion is a Federal style home mostly built in 1792 by Thomas Johnings Seth. It was later owned by Severn Teackle Wallis, a founding member of the Maryland Historical Society, in 1880. Located in Queenstown, the wing of this house is older, but it is unknown when it may have been built, adding to the mystique of the structure. Recorded ghost sightings go as far back as 1879 when the owner, Miss Sally Harris, and her guest, Mrs. Nancy De Courcy, heard a knock at the front door one night. When they, along with a servant, answered, the figure of William Sterrett, Miss Harris's deceased nephew, stood before them at the door. He walked inside and motioned for the ladies to follow. When he came to the door where he usually slept during his stays at Bloomingdale, he simply passed right through the closed door. The women unlocked the door and ventured inside to find only an unkempt bed as if someone had just been sleeping in it. William Sterrett was nowhere to be found.

2. Kent Manor Inn

The original building of Kent Manor Inn was built around 1820, with additions made in 1860. Its generous size has made it an ideal historic inn and restaurant. Room 209 has been particularly haunted with lights being turned on and off, incessant knocking, and the television abruptly being turned off. One of the staff saw a ghostly man sitting in room 303 and ran out screaming. Alexander Thompson, who owned the estate for a number of years in the 1800s and for whom nearby Thompson's Creek is named, has been seen a number of times riding a white horse up the drive to the house.

3. A Ghost Goes to Court!

In the late 1790s, Thomas Harris died and left his brother, James, the executor of his will. He had left instructions that the land should be sold by James and the money divided by his children. After James sold the property, it was discovered that Thomas had bought the land "in tail," meaning that the land ownership was limited to an individual and his or her direct descendants; however, James kept the money for himself. Two years later, James died and the children of Thomas sued the widow of James. Just before James passed away, William Briggs, a close friend to Thomas, told him that he'd received a message from the ghost of Thomas that James should "return the proceeds of the sale to the orphan's court." The case went to court and Briggs, a veteran of the American Revolution and known to have been of noble character, testified about his conversation with the ghost. Briggs told of a number of encounters with Harris, many of which Thomas did not speak. Finally, while busy in the field with a hand named Bailey, the ghost pulled Briggs aside and told him in a deep, low voice of the instructions for his brother. Bailey testified that he saw Briggs actively in conversation, but could see no one that Briggs could possibly be talking to. Unfortunately, the counsel for both the plaintiffs and defendants had already agreed before the trial that the money was unrecoverable and let William Briggs testify for show.

Somerset County

1. Cellar House Plantation

The Cellar House Plantation is shrouded in mystery. The current house was built in the 1730s on top of an old Indian burial ground and reportedly contains a trapdoor to a tunnel that leads out to the swamp, which was used to smuggle in goods. However, the first house on the site is believed to have been built in 1666 by a French sea captain as a gift to his wife. One day when he returned early from one of his voyages, he discovered his wife was having an affair with one of the locals. He threw her out of the house, but she made an attempt to return after she'd had the man's baby. She traveled by raft to Cellar House, but the raft capsized and the baby drowned. When the sea captain saw her pulling herself out of the water, he took no mercy upon her; he wrenched her up to the master bedroom and stabbed her to death. The sea captain fled and the woman's body was not found until months later. There were a number of people who claimed to have seen her imprint on the floor of the bedroom, but new floorboards have long since covered it up. Today, on cold and rainy nights, the drowned baby can be heard crying from the shore for its murdered mother. Discovery of a skeleton in the basement during restoration have led people to wonder if this was perhaps the remains of the woman, but it could also be that of an Indian from the burial ground.

2. Teackle Mansion

Dennis Littleton Teackle was one of the richest people in all of Somerset County when he built this Federal-style home. He supplied some of the lumber used to construct the U.S. Capitol building as well as a number of the day's Navy vessels. Most of his business was in trade, so his wealth fluctuated over the years. He sold Teackle Mansion in 1807, repurchased it in 1815, and then sold it again in 1839. When he died in 1848, he only had $25 left to his name. The mansion and its grounds were separated into three deeds, which made matters somewhat complicated later on. In the 1930s and 1940s, the mansion was divided into apartments, but a number of local residents sought to have the home restored to its former glory.

Putting the pieces together took some time as different fund-raising groups bought out different wings. Finally, in 2000, the entire mansion was brought back together for the first time in over 150 years. With more attention directed at the historic structure, reports of hauntings began to trickle in. A college student who interned at the mansion once awoke to the apparition of a woman floating in his room. She hasn't been seen since, but others claim that the spirit of Dennis Littleton Teackle roams the premises protecting his home.

3. Waterloo Country Inn

Henry Waggaman built this Georgian mansion in 1755, and his remains, as well as many of his descendants, rest on the premises in a small family graveyard. In 1864, the house began serving as the county Almshouse; now it is a historic bed and breakfast. Visitors of the inn have on occasion seen ghostly apparitions of the Waggaman family floating about the family graves.

St. Mary's County

1. Moll Dyer

Moll Dyer was an unsightly hermit woman who lived in a hut deep in the woods of St. Mary's County during the late 1600s. Given her demeanor, lifestyle, and the superstitions of the time, the local townspeople deemed her a witch. When bad storms hit or accidents happened, Moll was blamed. One bitter winter night, the community decided to run off Moll by burning down her hut. When they hadn't seen her for a few days, they figured she had moved on elsewhere and their problems were solved, but a boy playing in the woods came upon her frozen body kneeling in front of a large rock. One of her hands was raised while the other was frozen to the rock. After the discovery, strange accidents began to occur, storms ripped through the area, and people took ill. Upon the rock was discovered her ghostly handprint and, in 1972, the 875-pound rock was transplanted to St. Mary's County Historical Society in Leonardtown. Visitors inspecting the rock have experienced strange feelings and camera malfunctions. In other parts of the area, people have claimed to see the visage of Moll Dyer at night, and there's a local legend that on the coldest night of the year Moll will visit the location where her hut had been and the rock at which she died.

2. Point Lookout Light

At the very southern tip of St. Mary's county stands Point Lookout Light, a beacon for ships built in 1830, but better known these days as "America's Most Haunted Lighthouse." Point Lookout's existence has been shrouded in mysterious circumstances ever since it was first built. Just two months after construction finished, the first lighthouse keeper suddenly died. One keeper had the unfortunate luck of having a cat that broke in excess of twenty-five lamps and the keeper was denied his full pay.

After the Battle of Gettysburg, 10,000 Confederate prisoners were brought to Point Lookout and it was turned into a military prison known as Camp Hoffman. Over 45,000 more prisoners would eventually be transported under the lighthouse and almost 4,000 would ultimately die from their wounds, disease, and poor conditions. The most common type of apparition seen in the area is that of Civil War soldiers still performing their duty. Joseph Haney, an officer aboard the *Express* when it sank in the bay during a major storm in 1878, was seen at the back porch of the lighthouse almost one hundred years after his body had washed up on shore. This was reported by state park official Gerald J. Sword who lived in the lighthouse for a number of years and experienced a variety of unexplained incidents that included disembodied footsteps throughout the lighthouse, lights turning on and off, unexplained snoring, a glowing wall, and doors and objects banging about.

Famed ghost hunter Dr. Hans Holzer researched Point Lookout in the early 1980s and collected an assortment of mysterious voices using EVP, (Electric Voice Phenomenon) within the lighthouse and around the park. Some of these recordings included audible phrases such as, "my home," and, "fire if they get close to you." Ron and Nancy Stallings of the Maryland Committee for Psychical Research were involved in the research as well and were able to capture a photograph of a headless Confederate soldier leaning against a wall in the front bedroom.

3. Saint Andrew's Church Road Bridge

This bridge in St. Mary's County is haunted by two different ghosts.

⊛ The oldest likely comes from an old slave cabin near the bridge that used to house a young slave woman who harbored a great hatred for her master. She'd had enough of being made to sleep with him, so one night she decided to hit him with a frying pan and run away. Her plan went awry when she accidentally killed him with the blow to the head. She still ran, but she was hunted down the next day and killed near where the bridge now stands. Her ghost now causes minor accidents on the bridge as she jumps out into traffic apparently still trying to escape.

⊛ The other ghost involves a young woman whose husband had been away fighting in World War II. She'd become pregnant with their child before he'd left and he had yet to see his son. Just after the war ended, the woman received a phone call from her husband stating that he was in town and would be home shortly in a borrowed car. Impatiently, she wrapped up the baby and hurried down the road in hopes that she would catch her husband on the way to the house. She was rounding the sharp curve just before St. Andrew's Church Road Bridge when the car he was driving bore in from the other direction. He didn't see his wife and baby in time and the car impacted with the woman, killing her on the spot. The baby flew out of her arms and landed in the water never to be seen again. Since then, on dark, chilly nights, a young woman can be seen running around near the bridge in a frenzy while the cries of a baby emanate from the frigid waters below the side of the bridge.

Talbot County

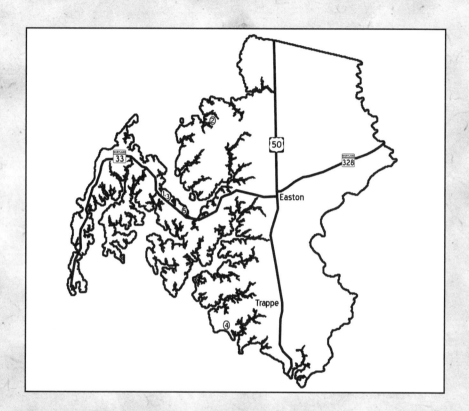

1. The Cannonball House

During the War of 1812, Mrs. Merchant was walking down the stairs with her baby daughter when a British cannonball blew through the roof of her St. Michaels home, rolled across the floor, and bounced down the stairs past the mother. Today the house resounds with thuds down the stairs in the form of invisible spirits. The padding of someone walking and disembodied footsteps have been heard in various places throughout the house.

2. Gross' Coate

Gross' Coate is a restored eighteenth century farmhouse built on the Eastern Shore. Although the land had been granted to

Roger Gross in 1658, the main center portion of the house was first built by William Tilghman in 1748. Three paintings by Charles Wilson Peale dating to 1790 once hung in the home. One depicted Richard Tilghman, the house's owner at that time; another his family; and the final one his sister, Mary. According to Hulbert Footner's *Rivers of the Eastern Shore*, in 1790 "It is related that Peale fell in love with Aunt Molly while staying at Gross' Coat and she with him. This is borne out by the exquisite delicacy and wistfulness depicted in Aunt Molly's young face. The proud brother would not hear of her marrying a middle-aged widower with children, and he locked her up until Peale was out of the house. As she eventually married beneath her anyhow, she might as well have been given to the celebrated artist. The unhappy Aunt Molly lived to a great age, and the light tapping of her stick is still heard late at night in the corridors." She's also been seen as a ghostly apparition floating down the stairs to unlock the front door. The Tilghmans were also a superstitious lot, and while there are a number of graves in the nearby family graveyard, there are only a few headstones. They believed that whoever erected a headstone for one of their beloved would be the next to pass away.

3. Kemp House

Colonel Joseph Kemp, a hero in the War of 1812, built this Federal-style house in 1807 in the town of St. Michaels. A young Robert E. Lee once stayed in the "Yellow Room" for two nights, but it's the "Blue Room" that is most known for its ghostly activity. During the daytime the room is generally serene, but at night guests have woken up to the rocking chair moving as if someone was in it watching them and at times the edge of the bed will sink down, similar to someone sitting there. Staff have come to call the spirit "Joseph" in honor of the original owner.

4. Kissing Ghost of the Wilderness

The Wilderness near Chlora's Point was built of white brick in 1785, with an addition added in 1810 by former Maryland governor Daniel Martin. There is a bedroom in the house in which when a man lays down to sleep he will be awoken by the deathly cold kiss of a female phantom. Hulbert Footner's 1944 *Rivers of the Eastern Shore* tells us, "It appears that one of the early Martin proprietors, upon returning home from a ride to inspect his farms, found that his young wife had died suddenly during his absence. The poor woman cannot rest quietly because she was deprived of an opportunity to bid her husband farewell, and any man who sleeps in the chamber where her husband used to lie, will be awakened in the night by the soft kiss of a beautiful young woman." Another story resounds from that same room in which a young woman was woken at night by a tall grinning man with a black mustache who floated about the room. When family members rushed to her aid after hearing her screams, they found her trapped in the bed with a rocking chair pressed down upon her. Matching her description, it is believed the man was J. Ramsey Spear, proprietor of the Wilderness during the 1930s.

5. Peg Alley's Point

The peninsula of Peg Alley's Point rests along the Miles River and is named for a tragedy that happened there many years ago. An oysterman from Baltimore had abandoned his wife and went to work with a group of men camping at the point. She found him at the camp and, after some discussion, the husband talked her into following him away from the others and into the brush. There he clubbed her to death. Since then, a number of people have seen her visage in the area. The most notable incident was that of a Mr. Kennedy, the employer of a group of rail-splitters working near the point. When his foreman had become scared off, Kennedy laughed at him and rode down to the location. His horse became suddenly agitated and he spotted a woman on a log that must have been the cause. Thin and sallow with jet-black hair and wearing a faded calico dress, she rose up from the log. Kennedy angrily called out for her to get out of the way so he could regain control of his horse. She turned from him, walked into the thicket, and disappeared.

Washington County

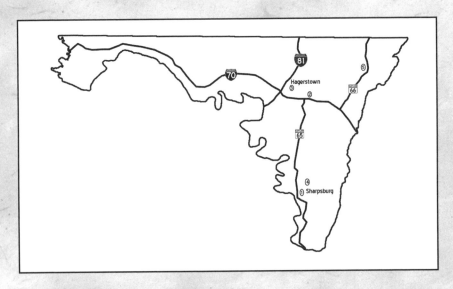

1. Antietam Battlefield

The Battle of Antietam on September 17, 1862, was the bloodiest one-day battle in American history, costing over 23,000 Americans their lives. While the battle itself was essentially a standoff, General Robert E. Lee, having already been chased across South Mountain by Union troops, retreated over the Potomac to Harper's Ferry, giving the North a pivotal victory. There are a number of different ghosts stemming from this infamous battlefield.

✤ "The Bloody Lane," where 5,000 soldiers lost their lives, has been known to still give off a whiff of gunpowder and some visitors have seen the apparitions of Rebels walking the lane. It is also the site of one of the site's stranger tales in which witnesses claimed they heard the Christmas carol "Deck The Halls" sung by invisible soldiers. What they likely heard was the Gaelic chant for "clear the way," which is "Faugh-a-balaugh" since the Union troops fighting at this location were the 69th Regiment of New York known as the "Irish Brigade."

❖ Burnside's Bridge, where General Ambrose Burnside pushed back the Confederates after a number of failed attempts, has been haunted by peculiar balls of blue light and the cadence of a drum beat.

❖ The Pry House, which stands on the battlefield, was used by Union General George McClelland as his headquarters during the battle and seems to be haunted by a female spirit. During restoration, an unknown woman in an 1800s dress was spotted walking down the staircase and then suddenly vanished.

❖ The Piper House, which served as Confederate General James Longstreet's Headquarters with its barn utilized as a field hospital, is now a bed and breakfast and has had peculiar reports of muffled voices, eerie sounds, and a ghostly apparition that has appeared in the bathroom doorway.

2 Chaney House

During the retreat from Gettysburg, the Confederate Army fought a diversionary battle in Funkstown while General Robert E. Lee's troops set up a nine-mile front from Williamsport to St. James. During the battle in which 479 soldiers were killed or wounded, many of the town's homes were used as makeshift hospitals. One of these was the Chaney House, now Ruth's Antiques. For a time, tenants had reported the sound of a piano playing periodically and the appearance of a woman in a Civil War nurse's dress. Since Ruth's Antiques has been in business, the hauntings have dramatically quieted down. However, a customer from the Midwest who had bought a table while shopping in passing claimed the table itself must have been haunted, because ever since the purchase...a Civil War nurse has haunted her house.

3. Hager House

In 1739, Jonathan Hager bought two hundred acres of land from Daniel Dulany and dubbed it "Hager's Fancy." The house he built upon it had its own protected water supply and, with its twenty-two-inch walls, was used at times as a frontier

Antietam National Battlefield in Sharpsburg.

fort during Indian attacks. Hager sold the house to Jacob Rohrer in 1745, and it remained in that family for almost two years. Now owned by the Washington County Historical Society, it has been opened as a museum for the public. Visitors sometimes see a rocking chair moving of its own accord and footsteps have been heard going up the stairs. Tour guides have reported a corncob doll that will move from place to place around the house and a dark figure that will appear on the porch and then vanish.

4. The Indian Maiden of Antietam Creek

This ghostly legend of Antietam Creek dates all the way back to 1750. A young local Indian girl fell in love with a boy who had just moved to the area with his family from Delaware. They were each only fifteen years old, but fell for each other hard and began meeting in secret regularly at the creek. One day the boy stopped coming and the young maiden was distraught. When she later found out he'd been killed in an accident, she took her own life in the creek. Since that time the young Indian girl's spirit can sometimes be seen paddling a canoe down the river calling out for her love.

5. Smithsburg

Nestled into the hills, Smithsburg already presents a sense of eeriness when its fog creeps in, but its ghosts heighten the effect. Many of the old country houses have crumbled to the ground, taking their secrets to the grave, but still present a feeling of foreboding. One such house was on Old Forge Road, but has since been burned to the ground. People who ventured in have spoken of the chill in the air, the feeling that someone was always watching them, and doors slamming behind them. The site still conjures up a sense of cold dread.

In another house dated before the Civil War, a mother and daughter tandem reside. The little girl had died of kidney failure before she was three and, as a ghost, has been known to try to climb into bed with people. Ever since and into her afterlife, the mother treated other small children as her own child, acting as a nanny to babies and small children in the house. She's tucked them in, replaced their pacifiers, and has been seen through the window of the nursery holding a baby.

Other Smithsburg ghosts include the occasional Civil War soldier and a few apparition sightings at Bond Farm Pond.

Wicomico County

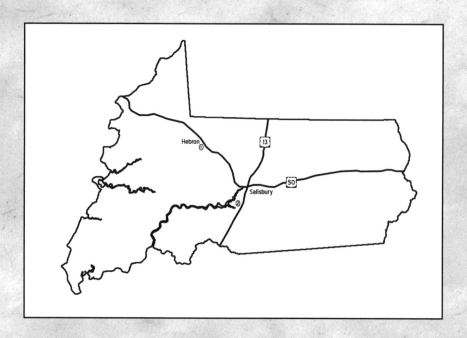

1. The Hebron Lights

Since 1952, the small town of Hebron has sparked the interest of ghost hunters and UFO seekers. It was then that two police officers chased a glowing ball of light down a dark country road just outside of the town until it finally disappeared. An official Maryland State Police report was filed and the incident made the news; however, citizens of Hebron had already been accustomed to the spheres. Many believe these glowing orbs to be the spirit of a slave that had been hanged, an old railroad worker with his lantern, or the victim of a nearby accident or murder. UFO aficionados believe it to be a sign of alien life while others think it must be marsh gas playing tricks. Whichever is true, many people still go out to try to catch a glimpse of the lights dancing down the country road.

2. Salisbury University

Salisbury University opened in 1925 as a two-year college on the Eastern Shore, but is now an accredited four-year comprehensive university. The oldest structure on the campus, Holloway Hall, features a classical bell tower and clock. A student who died while he attended Salisbury haunts the bell tower...his apparition can be seen at times on moonlit nights.

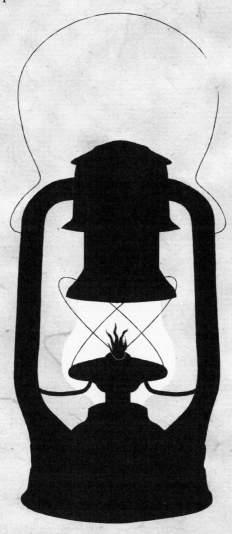

Worcester County

1. Furnace Town

The Nassawango Furnace just outside of Snow Hill was built in 1832 and around it grew the small village of Furnace Hill. The population swelled to as many as four hundred people in 1838 with one hundred homes, a general store, a blacksmith shop, a school, a church, and even a hotel. A dozen years later, the furnace closed down, unable to keep up with the competition out west, and the town disappeared. Today the site has been restored and is open to the public as the Furnace Town Living Heritage

Museum. The restoration project may have stirred the spirit of a slave named Sampson Hat, or he could well have been haunting the site for some time. Sampson was a slave who refused to leave the site of Furnace Town after it closed up; he continued to live there for a number of years. While he had made it quite clear that he wished to be buried there when he died, his wish was not granted and he was buried elsewhere. It is believed that it is his tall apparition that has been seen walking through the village at times, and was seen quite often during the restoration of the site.

2. The Heavy Bible

Locating the church where the legendary "Heavy Bible" resides is quite a task. There are those who claim it is in an old church near Bishopville. Some believe it used to rest in a church long since abandoned and has moved to the historic Furnace Town near Snow Hill. Yet another story places the Bible in a church in Cambridge. The common legend is that as one moves the Heavy Bible further and further from the pedestal on which it sits, it gets heavier and heavier. One story tells of two boys who tried to steal it and couldn't even lift it off the stand. On another occasion, a number of men

placed it in a wheelbarrow to take it from the church, but the further they got the heavier the wheelbarrow got. They decided to bring it back to the church and the closer they got the lighter the wheelbarrow became. The Cambridge story takes the Heavy Bible in a different direction, stating that the church had been overtaken by a cult and the only one that can actually move the Bible is the Devil.

3. Snow Hill Inn

The Snow Hill Inn was built in 1835 as a residence for a distinguished businessman named Levin Townsend. The building has operated in a number of capacities including a post office and a Mexican restaurant, but most recently it has served as an inn. From the 1870s until 1929, it was the home of the Aydelotte family, including Dr. John S. Aydelotte, Snow Hill's town doctor, and his son William James who committed suicide in a Baltimore boarding house at the young age of twenty-one while attending the University of Maryland's School of Pharmacology. There are debates even to this day as to whether William took his life because he had poor marks at school and thought he was going to be seen as a failure to his father, or whether a tenuous relationship with a woman from Westminster caused him too much anxiety, or even if another involved party murdered him. Now known as "J. J." to the tenants and visitors of the Snow Hill Inn, he spends his time locking doors, turning lights on and off, knocking on walls, rearranging objects on tables, and appearing briefly in mirrors. During the renovation into an inn, two men were working in a room and wished to open a window. No matter how hard they tried, they couldn't raise it at all. Reluctantly, they left it alone and went to work on other things in the room. Suddenly, the window flew up, terrifying the two men.

Bibliography

Baltimore Sun. "Barbara Fritchie." *Baltimore Sun*, April 24, 1875.

Bay Weekly Online. "Legends of Point Lookout." Bay Weekly Online, http://www.bayweekly.com/year00/issue8_42/lead8_42.html.

Bosarge, Mimi. "Ghost Chicks: Two Women Use Paranormal Talents, Modern Equipment to Explain Haunt." *The Black Vault*. Accessed at http://www.theblackvault.com/article-print-16801.html.

Bready, James H. *Baseball in Baltimore*. Baltimore, Maryland: The Johns Hopkins University Press, 1998.

Burgoyne, Mindie. "The Ghost of the Snow Hill Inn." *Writing the Vision*. Accessed at http://www.writingthevision.com/ghostofsnowhill.html.

Canon, Timothy and Nancy Whitmore. *Ghosts and Legends of Frederick County*. Frederick, Maryland: Studio 20, Inc., 2005.

Carter, Mike. "One Day I'll Have You!" *Hometown Annapolis*. Accessed at http://www.hometownannapolis.com/ha_feature.html.

Chalkly, Tom, Charles Cohen, and Brennen Jensen. "Charmed Afterlife." *City Paper*, October 25, 2000.

Crowe, Catherine. *The Night Side of Nature or Ghosts and Seers*. New York, New York: E.P. Dutton & Co., 1904.

Doss, Emily. "Local Ghost Stories Haunt Residents." *The Salisbury Flyer*, October 30, 2007.

Dunne, Patrick. "Ghost Stories Haunt Landon House." *The Gazette*, October 27, 2005.

Footner, Hulbert. *Rivers of the Eastern Shore*. Centreville, Maryland: Tidewater Publishers, 1970.

Gallagher, Trish. *Ghosts & Haunted Houses of Maryland*. Centreville, Maryland: Tidewater Publishers, 1988.

Glass, Jesse Jr. *Ghosts and Legends of Carroll County, Maryland*. Westminster, Maryland: Carroll County Public Library, 1998.

Hammond, John Martin. *Colonial Mansions of Maryland and Delaware*. Philadelphia, Pennsylvania: J. B. Lippincott Company, 1914.

Heidenreich, Chris. *Frederick: Local and American Crossroads*. Charleston, South Carolina: Arcadia Publishing, 2003.

Knauer, Carrie Ann. "Civil War-Era Painting Returns to Tavern." *Carroll County Times*, February 17, 2009.

Lake, Matt. *Weird Maryland*. New York, New York: Sterling Publishing Co., Inc., 2006.

Lang, Andrew. *Cock Lane and Common-Sense*. New York, New York: AMS Press, 1894.

Longfellow, Rickie. "Back in Time: Ghosts of Antietam's Battlefield and the Bloody Lane." U.S. Department of Transportation Federal Highway Administration. Accessed at http://www.fhwa.dot.gov/infrastructure/back1105.cfm.

Milford, Maureen. "Displacing Ghosts of Students and Sailors." *The New York Times*, March 12, 2000.

Mudd, Nettie. *The Life of Dr. Samuel A. Mudd*. New York, New York: Neale Publishing Company, 1906.

Okonowicz, Ed. *Haunted Maryland: Ghosts and Strange Phenomena of the Old Line State*. Mechanicsburg, Pennsylvania: Stackpole Books, 2007.

Picket News. "The Chaney House: Haunting of a Civil War Nurse." *Picket News*, October 26, 2008.

Rhodes, Jason. *Somerset County, Maryland: A Brief History*. Charleston, South Carolina: The History Press, 2007.

Rigaux, Pamela. "Walking With the Dead." *Frederick News-Post*, October 23, 2005.

Taylor, Troy. *Beyond the Grave: The History of America's Most Haunted Graveyards*. Decatur, Illinois: Whitechapel Press, 2001.
Ghost Hunter's Guidebook. Decatur, Illinois: Whitechapel Press, 2007.

Warfield, J.D. Founders of Anne Arrundel and Howard Counties, Maryland. Baltimore, Maryland: Kohn and Pollock, 1905.

Wooten, Orlando V. "Bloody Tales of Murder and Piracy Cloak Mystery of Old Cellar House." *The Daily Times*, October 13, 1966.

Index